British Diplomacy

Foreign Secretaries Reflect

British Diplomacy

Foreign Secretaries Reflect

edited by Graham Ziegner

POLITICO'S

First published in Great Britain 2007 by
Politico's Publishing Ltd, an imprint of
Methuen Publishing Ltd
11–12 Buckingham Gate
London
SW1E 6LB

10 9 8 7 6 5 4 3 2 1

A CIP catalogue record for this book is available from the British Library.

ISBN-10: 1-84275-163-8
ISBN-13: 978-1-84275-163-3

Typeset by SX Composing DTP, Rayleigh, Essex
Printed and bound in Great Britain by MPG Books, Bodmin, Cornwall

Contents

Preface

Only a select few have experienced the view of the world afforded to Her Majesty's Secretary of State for Foreign and Commonwealth Affairs. *British Diplomacy* gives the wider public a rare glance at this view, one first delivered as a series of lectures in 2003 at the London School of Economics and Political Science under the title 'Developments in British Diplomacy: Foreign Secretaries Reflect'. In the following pages you will find updated versions of these lectures, where the former Foreign Secretaries reflect on their time in office and some of the key questions and challenges they faced.

Each Foreign Secretary has grappled with the challenge of the European Union's gradual emergence as a key actor in the international arena, while the transformations brought about by the end of the Cold War have raised questions about the threats Britain faces. Managing Britain's relations in such a world has demanded an ever-increasing amount of travel on the part of the Foreign Secretary, some arguing that this has been at the expense of detailed and well considered policy-making. The increasing role of the Prime Minister in international and European affairs has raised questions about the role and autonomy of the Foreign Secretary. These and many other issues are touched on in the following pages by the former Foreign Secretaries.

In his introductory chapter, Professor William Wallace maps out the path of Britain's foreign policy from the early nineteenth century to the 1970s. In the following chapters it becomes clear that while the word 'crisis' is commonly heard, many of the issues a Foreign Secretary faces resurface time and again. Lord Carrington mentions the acrimonious discussions over the EU budget, as does Lord Howe. If Jack Straw were to have written a chapter for this book, it would have been surprising if he had not mentioned the budget negotiations which as Foreign Secretary he oversaw in 2005 and which were heralded as one of the great successes of the UK presidency of the European Union in the second half of that year. The other major success of this UK presidency was the agreement to launch accession negotiations with Turkey. This was ultimately the fruition of the UK's policy of pushing for EU enlargement, something that was already established when Lord Owen served as Foreign Secretary. Indeed, the issue of Europe is one that is to be found in each of the former Foreign Secretaries' reflections.

The end of the Cold War and the reunification of Europe raised difficult questions not only for UK foreign policy but for international relations in general. The passing of the bipolar world of East–West tensions and the emergence of a unipolar world did not make the conduct of foreign policy any easier. The horrors of the former Yugoslavia and the growing process of globalisation brought to the fore such issues as humanitarian intervention, sovereignty, human rights and international justice. These are touched on, in particular, by Geoffrey Howe and Douglas Hurd.

Amongst this turbulence the centrality afforded to the relationship with the USA in UK foreign policy might have been expected to remain steady. Yet this relationship has also experienced its share of ups and downs, something Sir Malcolm Rifkind considers. And in their concluding chapter, Professor Christopher Hill and Tim Oliver outline a number of foreign policy challenges New Labour has faced, most notably the nature of the transatlantic relationship.

It would not have been possible to publish this book without the unfailing help of many colleagues and friends. First and foremost I would like to thank the former Foreign Secretaries who agreed to participate in this project, for the time they kindly gave up to prepare and deliver their lectures. In particular I would like to thank Lord Hurd, whose support from the very start was central to the project. I would like to thank Professor William Wallace for his lucid introduction and Professor Christopher Hill and Tim Oliver for their analysis of New Labour's foreign policy. Both these texts were specially written for this book and the combination of these texts and the lectures will give any student of British foreign policy a rapid introduction and overview combined with unique insights into many of the most important events in British diplomacy.

At the LSE I would like to thank the directors, Professor Lord Giddens (1997–2003) and Sir Howard Davies (2003 onwards) for their support of the project. They were instrumental in helping to organise the series and in supporting the publication of the book. Additionally, I would like to thank Margot Light, William Wallace, Christopher Hill, Maurice Fraser and John Kent for each chairing one of the lectures.

A special note of thanks goes to my former colleagues in the LSE Conference and Events Office. Their wholehearted encouragement and practical support helped make the project a reality. Both managers of the office, Gary Delaney and Alan Revel, did everything to ensure the smooth running of the project. Many other colleagues in the Conference and Events Office and other offices around the school helped ensure the lecture series ran smoothly. I would like to extend my warm thanks to Shona Macfarlane, Kylie Weston, Daniel Print, Rachel Ward, Judith Higgin, Jessica Winterstein, Nigel Stead, Beverley Friedgood and the many stewards who worked on the events.

Peter Tummons, Alan Gordon Walker and Jonathan Wadman at Politico's have been very helpful, encouraging and patient during the publication process. I am grateful for their comments on the final text. I would also like to thank Veda Poon for looking at some of the text and providing feedback. Last but not least I would like to thank my parents for their support throughout my time at university and for always encouraging me in the many projects in which I was involved.

Graham Ziegner
Brussels, November 2006

Introduction: Foreign Secretaries and Foreign Policy

William Wallace

The classic era in which to be a British Foreign Secretary was in the mid-
to late nineteenth century. England (as London politicians thought about
the four-nation state they governed) was at the centre of a great empire,
and played a key role in the diplomatic politics of the great European
powers. Foreign policy *was* diplomacy, conducted largely by a small core
of professional diplomats from a small number of major states. Trade
matters intervened from time to time, as in the Anglo-French commercial
treaty of 1860; military questions followed from the breakdown of
diplomacy. Financial questions might occasionally intervene, when some
state marginal to the European system failed to service the debts they had
unwisely shouldered to European banks; but then the Ottoman or
Egyptian or Chinese customs services would be put under British or other
'civilised' state tutelage. The Bank of England was not only independent
but privately owned, the Treasury concerned in international questions
only with the strains that expeditionary forces placed on the national
finances. A handful of Foreign Office officials, sharing what is now
the Foreign Office courtyard with the separate Indian and Colonial
Offices, advised the Foreign Secretary, corresponding with a diplomatic
service abroad that was drawn from the same multilingual elite.

Even then, the shadow of the Prime Minister hung over successive Foreign Secretaries. At the Congress of Vienna, in 1815, His Majesty's Government had been ably represented by Viscount Castlereagh, working alongside his fellow foreign ministers. At the Congress of Berlin in 1878, however, Lord Salisbury as Foreign Secretary was accompanied by his Prime Minister, Benjamin Disraeli, ennobled two years earlier as the 1st Earl of Beaconsfield. William Gladstone as Liberal leader famously campaigned on the Bulgarian massacres; Disraeli as Prime Minister was an avowed imperialist with an active interest in international politics. Nevertheless, by and large the direction of foreign policy remained slightly apart from domestic politics, a semi-detached aspect of the business of government. Crown prerogative remained a significant factor, limiting parliamentary oversight of diplomatic business – though the scale of some inquiries into overseas expeditions and international incidents after the event, and the wealth of published material, was remarkable by today's standards. The monarch herself, closely related to many of the other crowned heads of European states, took an active interest in international diplomacy; personal relations among heads of state, as now among heads of government, might after all affect political relations.

Heads of state and government took over from the diplomats at the Versailles peace conference of 1919. Only David Lloyd George had the standing to negotiate with Georges Clemenceau and President Woodrow Wilson; and only Lloyd George had the standing at home to sell the peace terms agreed to an exhausted and embittered electorate. From now on, Foreign Secretaries relied on their special relationship with the Prime Minister: a partnership (as Geoffrey Howe describes his relationship with Margaret Thatcher, many years later) in which the political skills, as well as the political priorities, of the two office holders shaped the way they worked together. The professional Foreign Office preferred to work to its own minister, without interference from other departments. But the Committee on Imperial Defence, established (under the chairmanship of the Prime Minister) in 1904, had started a gradual process of interdepartmental co-ordination, in which the Foreign Office had to negotiate with other stakeholders in overseas policy. Lloyd George's 'garden suburb' of advisers working to him from huts behind 10 Downing Street encroached further into the Foreign Office's distinctive domain. A degree of normality, and autonomy, appeared to be returning under succeeding governments in the 1920s and early 1930s – though international recession, financial imbalances and competitive measures of protection brought the economic departments more directly into foreign policy. But governments abroad were falling under autocratic leaders, conducting their own foreign and domestic policies, with foreign ministers as clear subordinates. Neville Chamberlain, in responding to the challenges posed by Hitler and Mussolini, preferred to lean on Sir Horace Wilson for advice, rather than on a Foreign Office suspected of anti-German prejudice. It was Chamberlain himself, as head of government, who went to Munich, leaving Anthony Eden as Foreign Secretary to protest and resign.

Winston Churchill and Ernest Bevin formed a real wartime partnership, partly based upon Bevin's ability to represent working-class loyalty to the international strategy of the coalition government. But it was Churchill who forged the personal relationship with Franklin D. Roosevelt, and found the rhetoric that defined the 'Special Relationship' and linked the 'English-speaking peoples'. Wartime leaders necessarily gather together the strands of domestic and foreign policy into their hands; wartime summitry, from the western Atlantic to Tehran to Yalta, concentrated authority further. Postwar reconstruction revived the autonomy of the Foreign Secretary and the Foreign Office. Bevin, with his huge prestige within the Labour movement as well as his wealth of wartime experience, commanded exceptional respect within the government; if he said that the Durham miners would not accept the Schuman plan to bring together the coal and steel industries of western European countries, the rest of the Cabinet accepted his judgement.

The Suez watershed

For all of the contributors who follow, Suez was the greatest watershed in post-war British foreign policy: an event that impressed itself on all of the rising generation entering politics. Before Suez, Britain could still claim to be a great power, the partner of the United States in leadership of the free world. After Suez, it was possible only to be a junior partner, with resource constraints pinning down global ambitions and forcing retreat from colonial territories and overseas bases. Before Suez, Britain saw its interests stretching across the Middle East – where it remained the dominant external power – to Aden, east Africa, Singapore and Hong Kong. After Suez, it was difficult to resist American pressure to come to terms with Britain's European position, and accept that we should share our sovereignty with our neighbours through joining the developing institutions of the EEC. The Special Relationship with the United States, determinedly re-established by Harold Macmillan in 1957, was from then on clearly a subordinate relationship, in which British governments hoped to influence American policy in return for offering loyal support to its strategic direction, and from which they gained in return additional international prestige, intelligence, and nuclear co-operation.

The management of British foreign policy had been weak in the years that preceded the 1956 Suez crisis and intervention. Both Prime Minister and Foreign Secretary – Winston Churchill and Anthony Eden – were ageing and intermittently unwell; Churchill was incapacitated by a stroke for several months in 1954. British policy was committed to retaining great-power status, even though the costs were rising and the obstacles increasing. Britain's position in Iran had been shaken by the nationalisation of Anglo-Iranian Oil in 1950 and was restored in the Anglo-American coup of 1953 only with substantial US support. British forces had been withdrawn from the Canal Zone in 1954. US briefing for their British allies of the massive destructive power of their first hydrogen bomb tests pushed the British government into a major and costly programme of their own, which conducted its first successful test in 1957. Keeping abreast of the United States also meant investment in technologically advanced weapons, from long-range bombers to missiles; the resulting diversion of scientific and engineering skills from other sectors of industry, and the acute strain on government finances, brought the Treasury and the Board of Trade actively into play. It was economic weakness that undermined the Suez intervention. American refusal to support the pound on international exchanges was enough to force a retreat, since the size of the 'sterling balances' – debts accumulated during the war and since – left the pound sterling as an international currency vulnerable to attack once confidence was shaken.

Macmillan as Prime Minister was the conjuror who masterminded the illusion of continuing great-power status, while quietly dismantling those elements that could no longer be afforded. He recognised that the Anglo-American Special Relationship must be rebuilt, but could only be rebuilt on a more subordinate basis, with subordination disguised by close personal relations. He had, after all, worked with General Dwight D. Eisenhower as British minister in north Africa during the war; his later relationship with John F. Kennedy started from personal wartime links between the two families (through the Cavendishes, the family of the Dukes of Devonshire). In Macmillan's active summit diplomacy, travelling between Washington and Moscow and claiming on occasion to mediate between the two, his own Foreign Secretary was very much a junior partner. Selwyn Lloyd, who had succeeded Macmillan as Foreign Secretary when Macmillan became Chancellor of the Exchequer in December 1955, was the executor of prime ministerial foreign policy from 1957 to 1960.

Macmillan attempted to balance Churchill's 'three circles' of British international influence: the Special Relationship with the United States, Britain's leading role within what was then described as 'the British Commonwealth and Empire', and our military and political commitment to our European allies. He also attempted to bridge the widening gap between aspirations and resources, by turning to the United States, or more hesitantly to France, to share in common weapons programmes or to provide advanced technology. The Bermuda agreement, in 1957, re-established US–UK co-operation on nuclear weapons, in return for implicit understandings about the acceptance of American international leadership and extended access to British bases and intelligence resources. Unfortunately, first the Eisenhower and then the Kennedy administrations wanted Britain to fit into their 'grand design' for a two-pillar Atlantic partnership by entering the infant EEC. It was the shortfall in high technology and the continuing commitment to the Commonwealth that brought Macmillan down. Washington's cancellation of Skybolt, the stand-off missile which the UK had ordered for its next-generation nuclear deterrent, forced him to use all his charm on President Kennedy, this time in the Bahamas, to gain the promise of Polaris, after a summit with President Charles de Gaulle marked by mutual misunderstanding.

Foreign policy in the 1950s was conducted not only by the Foreign Secretary but by two other secretaries of state, with the Commonwealth Office and the Colonial Office staffed by separate services and managing policy towards the British Commonwealth and Empire. What is now the Foreign Office courtyard had originally housed the India Office and the Colonial Office as well as the Foreign Office itself, its splendid range of offices running from halfway along Downing Street round the corner to face St James's Park. Oliver Lyttelton, Alexander Lennox-Boyd and Ian Macleod, as Colonial Secretaries in the 1950s, handled successive negotiations with colonies in Africa and Asia moving towards independence, including the establishment of the Central African Federation as an attempt to reconcile white rule in Southern Rhodesia with black majority rule in Northern Rhodesia and Nyasaland (now Zimbabwe, Zambia and Malawi respectively). A succession of Tory peers, from Lord Ismay to the Earl of Home (later Foreign Secretary and, as Sir Alec Douglas-Home, Prime Minister), managed relations with 'the white Commonwealth' and the Asian dominions. But it was Macmillan again, as Prime Minister, who altered the balance of British policy in Africa in his 'wind of change' speech to the South African Parliament, in February 1960.

Macmillan's other strategic shift, in 1960–1, was to open negotiations with the European Economic Community, partly in response to sustained American pressure, partly in recognition of the rising importance of economic links with continental Europe and the declining economic importance of the Commonwealth. Here, however, he clothed the high politics of European commitment in the low politics of commercial negotiations, entrusting the British negotiating team to the Board of Trade. Edward Heath carried the negotiations forward, with other ministers anxious about their implications for agricultural subsidies and prices, for relations with the Commonwealth and for the unity of the Conservative Party. Negotiations in the autumn of 1962 were bogged down in the details of concessions for New Zealand butter and Australian pineapple chunks, giving President de Gaulle the political opportunity to break them off without arousing bitter hostility from other member governments. Alongside this, the Prime Minister had tried to adjust the strategic balance of British foreign policy through successive bilateral summits with de Gaulle. The American decision to cancel Skybolt, followed by the Cuban missile crisis, upset the delicate and deliberately ambiguous balance that Macmillan was attempting. He travelled first to Rambouillet, then to Nassau, succeeding in his objective to secure Polaris missiles as an alternative basis for the British nuclear deterrent, but at the cost of convincing suspicious Gaullists that Britain remained an American ally first, unready to make a political commitment to European integration. British diplomats and embassies played active roles in all of these foreign policy manoeuvres; but the Foreign Secretary himself was a subordinate player.

'A major power of the second rank'

The collapse of negotiations to enter the EEC also led to the collapse of the Kennedy administration's 'Grand Design' for a two-pillar Atlantic Community, with Britain a leading power within an enlarged but compliant European pillar. The three circles of British foreign policy seemed in 1963–4 to be coming apart. The assassination of John F. Kennedy, and the replacement of Harold Macmillan by Alec Douglas-Home, weakened the personal warmth that had held the transatlantic relationship closely together. The EEC moved forward towards a common agricultural policy that was structurally disadvantageous to British agriculture; it also negotiated as a bloc with the United States in the GATT 'Kennedy round', across Britain's weaker negotiating position. In southern Africa, the Central African Federation had been dismantled, leaving the problem of the white minority in Southern Rhodesia, resisting British pressure to make concessions before they were granted independence, to preoccupy a now-multiracial Commonwealth.

The Labour government that came uncertainly into power in 1964, with a majority of three seats, thus inherited a foreign policy in which the gap between claims to great-power status and the multilateral networks and economic resources needed to substantiate that claim had widened dangerously. Labour ministers, deeply conscious that their devaluation of the pound in 1947 had been presented by the Conservatives as a betrayal of Britain's national standing and a mark of economic incompetence, were determined to maintain its value, in spite of the overhang of sterling debts and a continuing trade deficit. They were also conscious that the Conservatives would try to portray them as unpatriotic if they cut back on defence expenditure; they therefore attempted to maintain the deployment of British forces 'east of Suez', with bases in Aden, the Persian Gulf and Singapore. Their majority shrank rapidly to one when the foreign secretary, Patrick Gordon Walker, who had lost his seat at the general election, failed also to win the by-election intended to bring him back into Parliament. This fragile government felt unable to respond firmly to Rhodesia's unilateral declaration of independence, leaving the problem of negotiating the transition to black majority rule to its Conservative successors fifteen years later.

Eighteen months later, in March 1966, the Labour Party won a sufficiently convincing majority at a second general election to give it a greater degree of freedom in foreign affairs. But the dilemmas of strategic balance and inadequate resources remained acute. Harold Wilson as Prime Minister and Michael Stewart as Foreign Secretary (from 1965 to 1966 and again from 1968 to 1970) managed skilfully to resist American pressures to contribute British forces to support the USA in Vietnam, using to the full the argument that British military operations in the Malaysian 'confrontation' with Indonesia were part of the same global struggle. After the 1966 election, George Brown was appointed Foreign Secretary to explore with continental governments – most of all with the French – the possibility of relaunching an application to join the EEC. Joint leadership of this initiative by the Prime Minister and the Foreign Secretary this time made it explicit that this was a political and strategic exercise, with Wilson offering Britain's 'technological dowry' to Europe as an incentive to accept the UK. Charles de Gaulle, however, still preferred a smaller EEC under French leadership to a larger entity built around Franco-British partnership. The Franco-British Concorde project was carried all the way to completion, partly because British ministers discovered that the contract had made cancellation very costly; but the French cancelled other military aircraft schemes, and British companies were to withdraw from the French-led Airbus project at the end of the decade – to return later as junior partners. Britain's second application was announced in May 1967, and dismissed by de Gaulle in November.

The devaluation of the pound in the same month was, however, as significant a blow to British foreign policy, above all to its claim still to be a global power. The costs of maintaining bases and forces east of

Suez, with the increasingly expensive weapons systems required both to maintain Britain's position as a leading member of NATO in defending western Europe and to project forces across the world at long range, were beyond the capability of a state with an economy growing more slowly than its continental neighbours, and with a rising trade deficit. The Treasury now forced withdrawal from east of Suez. The Aden base had already been rendered untenable by local attack. The Malaysian confrontation with Indonesia had ended in 1964; the Singapore base was now to close by 1970. Only in the Persian Gulf were the small states that had once been India Office protectorates reluctant to see British forces withdraw – leaving them to seek American protection from their predatory neighbours.

Withdrawal of forces from global deployment left British leadership of the Commonwealth as the most important symbol of continuing status beyond western Europe and the north Atlantic. Sadly, the legacy of white rule in southern Africa, and the transformation of the Commonwealth from a club of 'white' dominions to a far larger group of recently independent states, had also created difficulties for Britain. South Africa had withdrawn, after Macmillan's warning speech, in 1961; but the issue of Rhodesia still hung over meetings, with the Nigerian government and its African partners holding British ministers responsible for a territory over which they exercised no effective control. Commonwealth Secretaries, and Prime Ministers at Commonwealth summits, were faced with demands that they should do more to enforce their formal responsibilities. When difficulties occurred elsewhere within the Commonwealth, however, other members were much less willing to share responsibilities. Uganda's expulsion of its Asian middle class, in 1968, brought a surge of refugees to Britain – and provoked domestic opposition. The governments of India and Pakistan, however, from whose territories their parents and grandparents had come, refused to accept that they should share in providing asylum. The advent of charter flights in the early 1960s had brought direct migration from south Asia to Britain on a large scale, to supplement post-war immigration from Britain's Caribbean territories. The Commonwealth on Britain's streets was a less unambiguously positive symbol for British Conservatives and the right-wing press than it had been when British ministers could claim to lead a quarter of the world's population.

The structure of Whitehall gradually adjusted to the transformation of the Commonwealth and the path to independence followed by most of Britain's remaining colonies. The shrinking Colonial Office lost its responsibilities for economic development to a new Department for Technical Co-operation in 1961, a more appropriately named body for managing assistance to newly independent territories. The Labour government in 1964 upgraded this into the Ministry of Overseas Development, to mark the greater importance it granted to international economic development; since then the ministry has moved in and out of the Foreign Office framework with successive changes of government. In 1966 the Colonial Office was absorbed into the Commonwealth Relations Office, which was in turn merged with is neighbour into the Foreign and Commonwealth Office (FCO) in 1968. It took another decade or more before the separate services were effectively integrated – ex-Commonwealth Office officials with Swahili or Urdu now working alongside Foreign Office Arabists and Russian experts. The FCO now occupied the whole of the quadrangle round the Foreign Office courtyard, once-grand offices grown decrepit by the late 1960s, with the Locarno rooms still suffering from their wartime occupation as an intelligence outstation; gradually, over the following thirty years, they were restored to their former glory, within buildings re-equipped with the computer cabling and office redesign needed for contemporary business. The new FCO had a large contingent of ministers of state and parliamentary secretaries, allocated regional and functional responsibilities to reduce the Foreign Secretary's burden of travel and meetings with visitors. The senior minister of state worked in the old Dominions Office, with its Map Room detailing the territories that Britain had once ruled; another room overlooked the Durbar Court of the former India Office, now roofed over as a space for receptions.

A quieter revolution in the management of foreign policy was also under way during the 1960s, driven by developments in travel and communications. The role of British embassies had traditionally been to represent His or Her Majesty's Government abroad, across the whole range of British interests. Increasing speed and ease of international travel, however, with the introduction of jet aircraft, allowed ministers and officials to travel to foreign capitals themselves, especially within western Europe and across the Atlantic – bringing an increasing number of ministers with formally domestic responsibilities into international negotiations between the British and other governments, and short-circuiting the intermediary role of embassies.

Even more radical in its impact was the introduction of direct dialling for international telephone calls. In the 1950s officials in domestic ministries had required the permission of the Foreign Office, through their own permanent secretary, before entering into direct communications with their counterparts within other governments. Well before the formal revolution of British entry to the EEC in 1973 the intermediary role of the Foreign Office and embassies had broken down;[1] once you could pick up the phone and call your opposite number without delay or immense expense, informal contacts proliferated. Multilateral organisations with regular meetings had given ministers and officials from 'home departments' direct acquaintance with their opposite numbers in other governments, visiting Paris for economic discussions within the Organisation for Economic Co-operation and Development (OECD) or (until Charles de Gaulle expelled it to Brussels in 1966) NATO; Basle for the Bank for International Settlements; Geneva, Rome, New York or Washington for meetings within global institutions. The widening agenda for intergovernmental consultation, now covering not only international economic and financial management but also scientific co-operation and exchange, health, labour standards and human rights, and a trade agenda slowly extending into technical and regulatory barriers to trade, brought much of Whitehall directly into the international arena for which the Foreign Office and its embassies had acted as gatekeepers.

So the Labour government reconsidered the legacy of grand embassies, diplomats, secure radio communications, Queen's Messengers transporting diplomatic bags, the British Council and the BBC World Service, the Commonwealth Development Corporation and the overseas aid agencies that it had inherited from Britain's imperial past. As part of the post-devaluation review of British external commitments and costs, a review committee was established, under the chairmanship of Sir Val Duncan, the chairman of Rio Tinto Zinc. Its report, in 1969, distinguished between the patterns of representation and policy-making needed in the 'inner' area of British foreign policy – the OECD and NATO world of industrial democracies with which relations were broad and intense – and those 'outer' areas where traditional representation was needed to maintain and report on relations less central to British interests. It recommended substantial reductions in the volume of traditional diplomatic reporting, criticised the FCO and several home departments for their resistance to closer cooperation, particularly in the staffing of overseas missions within the 'inner' area, and recommended changes in recruitment to open up the diplomatic service to a wider intake. But it was a phrase that it used about Britain's position in the world that aroused outrage in the conservative press – that Britain was now 'a major power of the second rank'. Thirteen years after the Suez intervention, two years after the forced devaluation and the decision to withdraw from east of Suez, there were still many who refused to accept that Britain was no longer a world power.

Britain in Europe

The Conservative government that – almost to its own surprise – won the 1970 election had drawn the conclusion that there was no effective alternative to reasserting its application for EEC membership. Edward

Heath, who had led the negotiations for Britain's first application in 1961–3, now became Prime Minister. As leader of the opposition, in 1969, he had given a series of lectures at Harvard that had set out a British foreign policy less closely integrated with the United States and more closely aligned with the European continent. Charles de Gaulle had resigned in mid-1969, three months after he had made an ambiguous offer to Sir Christopher Soames, then British ambassador in Paris, of Franco-British partnership in leading a more inter-governmental Europe. The EEC summit that followed his departure, at the Hague in December 1969, had led to agreement among the six member governments to reopen negotiations with the British, in return for entrenching agriculture spending within the common budget and for relaunching the Gaullist proposal for 'European political co-operation' (EPC) on foreign policy.

With the United States increasingly distracted by Vietnam and by domestic opposition to Vietnam, the Conservative government of 1970–4 focused primarily on European diplomacy. The team which negotiated EEC entry was drawn from most of the major departments in Whitehall, though with a strong FCO contingent. Franco-British negotiations on the political context were conducted between Prime Minister and President (Georges Pompidou); the personal chemistry between two essentially private and reserved political leaders appears to have helped to push detailed negotiations forward. They even extended to an attempted negotiation on co-operation between the two states' nuclear deterrent forces – popularly known within the British Ministry of Defence as 'the cornflake talks', because it proved so difficult to move beyond discussions of food and resupply for nuclear submarines to more substantive issues.

Even before the United Kingdom formally joined the EEC, in January 1973, the British Foreign Secretary, Sir Alec Douglas-Home, and his officials had begun to take part in the developing procedures of EPC: quarterly meetings of foreign ministers, which rapidly became more frequent, preparatory meetings of 'political directors', attended by a senior under-secretary, and a growing number of working groups. West European acceptance of the Soviet proposal for a Conference on Security and Co-operation in Europe gave this new procedure a focus, with detailed proposals and negotiating positions to be agreed among participants. When Labour succeeded the Conservatives in office in 1974, the additional informal meetings of foreign ministers that began, under German presidency, at Gymnich helped to reconcile the new Foreign Secretary to European integration; these discussions, he explained to an off-the-record meeting in 1975, built personal relationships and eased delicate trade-offs among governments.

With full membership, the British Foreign Secretary also became a member of the EEC Council of Ministers, in its most frequent formation as the General Affairs Council, meeting with his colleagues from other member states every few weeks, underpinned by bilateral conversations in different national capitals between meetings. These, together with NATO ministerial meetings, occasional ministerial meetings of the Western European Union, annual autumn sessions in New York at the beginning of each UN General Assembly, tours to other continents, attendance with the Prime Minister at biennial Commonwealth summits, and accompanying the Queen as head of state on state visits, added up to a gruelling overseas travel schedule for future Foreign Secretaries. Douglas Hurd once welcomed his French counterpart to a meeting with the comment that this was the fifth time they had met in two weeks, and in the fourth different city; Geoffrey Howe claimed that he saw his opposite numbers from France and Germany more often than his colleagues in the British Cabinet. But this required a strong physique; the strain of constant travel, at a time when another Labour government with a tenuous majority needed every minister to vote in the Commons on key issues, contributed to the early death in office of Anthony Crosland, in 1977.

Multilateral diplomacy through EPC contributed to the crisis in transatlantic relations of 1973–4 and to its resolution. Henry Kissinger, now the US Secretary of State, had announced a 'Year of

Europe' in a speech in April 1973, responding to the development of European co-operation in foreign policy with a demand that this should be safely rooted within the Atlantic alliance, with American officials fully engaged. British diplomats attempted to mediate between the French and the Americans, taking the lead in drafting a declaration on 'European identity' in foreign policy; but their balancing act was derailed by the October 1973 Arab–Israeli war and its aftermath, including the decision of the Copenhagen European Council in December 1973 to initiate a 'Euro–Arab dialogue' between EEC governments and the Arab League. The FCO at that point was operating partly by candlelight, as the oil embargo by the Organization of Petroleum Exporting Countries and a domestic coal strike reduced Britain to a three-day week. In February 1974 the weakened Conservative government gave way to a weak Labour government, its tenuous majority only marginally increased through a second election in October. James Callaghan, a powerful figure in his own right within the Labour Party as well as the new Foreign Secretary, led in resolving the transatlantic dispute, within the NATO framework.

Not for the first or the last time, Labour came into office in 1974 with a certain suspicion of the institutional FCO and the diplomatic service that staffed it: drawn from a limited social group; spending much of their careers outside Britain, their children subsidised to attend private boarding schools; out of touch with the people who had voted in a Labour government. After a parliamentary committee's criticisms of the high costs of a new residence for the British ambassador in Paris, an internal paper from the Cabinet Office's Central Policy Review Staff (CPRS), leaked in the *Daily Mail* of 29 December 1975, accused the FCO of 'perpetuating an elitist cadre, lavishing perks and privileges on its staff on a scale unknown elsewhere'. Callaghan, with the Prime Minister's approval, therefore announced a full CPRS study of British overseas representation, published (as the Berrill report) in 1977 – by which time he had himself become Prime Minister. Its radical proposals for merging the diplomatic service into the home civil service, integrating diplomats with staff in other ministries working on international issues to ensure that the balance of their careers allowed them more time in Britain, aroused a storm of protest from those affected and was not implemented. However, it marked the declining prestige of the FCO and its 'mandarins' within Whitehall, as other ministries became more and more engaged in direct intergovernmental relations, and as the power of the Cabinet Office and the Prime Minister grew.

The lectures that follow reflect the context that faced successive Foreign Secretaries from then on: within the EEC (from 1992 the EU), but not entirely happy within it; clinging to the Special Relationship with the USA, but not always confident that British support was rewarded with appropriate consultation and influence; unable to shrug off the remaining legacies of empire, from Rhodesia/Zimbabwe to the Falkland Islands and Hong Kong; struggling to retain influence within Whitehall against the centralising tendencies of the Prime Minister and the encroachment of other departments; inhibited by the echoes in public opinion of nostalgia for past great-power status and Protestant suspicions of Catholic continental Europe. Margaret Thatcher, as a radical from outside the traditional ruling class, shared Labour's entrenched mistrust for the FCO; it existed, she was reported as saying, to represent foreigners rather than to stand up for British interests. Personal relations between Foreign Secretary and Prime Minister, as well as between Foreign Secretary and opposite numbers within the governments of Britain's closest partners and between the Prime Minister and her closest foreign *interlocuteurs*, were vital factors in determining success or failure, as the lectures show. But that was not entirely new; personal factors had always played a large part in diplomacy and in relations among the senior members of a British government. It was the bureaucratic task that faced a Foreign Secretary in the 1980s and 1990s, balancing among bilateral and multilateral meetings overseas and interdepartmental negotiations at home, that their predecessors of a generation or two before would have found least familiar, and most exhausting.

The Rt Hon. the Lord Owen CH

Foreign Secretary February 1977–May 1979

'The ever-growing dominance of No. 10 in British diplomacy since 5 April 1982'

Based on a lecture given at the London School of Economics and Political Science, 8 October 2003

On Monday 5 April 1982 the personal decision of the Foreign Secretary, Peter Carrington, to resign, following the Argentine invasion of the Falkland Islands, was announced. As he wrote in his memoirs, 'The anger of the British people and Parliament at the Argentine invasion of the Falklands was a righteous anger, and it was my duty and fate to do something to assuage it.'[1]

This principled resignation had far-reaching consequences because Lord Carrington, stepping down, opened the way for Margaret Thatcher to take a quantum step in the weakening of the power and influence of the Secretary of State for Foreign and Commonwealth Affairs. It also started an institutional and political build-up of the role of No. 10 in the conduct of UK foreign and security policy at the expense of the Foreign Office and the Ministry of Defence. There followed two periods in which collective Cabinet government was devalued: 1982–1990, when Margaret Thatcher totally dominated discussion in the Cabinet and the Foreign Secretary's and Defence Secretary's powers were diminished; and 1997–2006, when Tony Blair's much-shortened Cabinet meetings took place and discussion happened as over Iraq, so that the form was observed but the practice completely changed. The key decisions were taken by the Prime Minister, sometimes with a few selected Cabinet ministers being involved.

Cabinet government is bound to differ under different Prime Ministers. Inevitably it is affected by their personality, the extent of their dominance in their party and many other factors. James Callaghan believed, and acted on the basis of that belief, that the Prime Minister, the Chancellor of the Exchequer, the Foreign and the Home Secretary

A version of this chapter was first published in the December 2003 issue of *Prospect* magazine, www.prospect-magazine.co.uk.

should never go to Cabinet differing on an issue without trying first to resolve any disagreement amongst themselves. In 1977, to take a specific example, I wanted a Commonwealth peacekeeping force, rather than a UN force, to implement the Anglo-American plan for Rhodesia. The Prime Minister, aware that Denis Healey, along with Tony Benn, was going to argue for the UN, rang me up to warn me and gave me the opportunity to change my recommendation in the Cabinet paper, which had not yet been sent out, saying he could not push a Commonwealth force through if, as he suspected, Denis had significant support. I chose to go ahead and was defeated and, though the UN was chosen, wrongly, because it was the weaker option, I had no cause for complaint. It was not an issue which the Prime Minister should have felt obliged to force through Cabinet.

Cabinet is not just about consulting Cabinet colleagues or an inner cabinet. It is involving the government departments at every appropriate level through their ministers, who can draw on past experience – in the case of Rhodesia, Denis Healey's six years as Defence Secretary entitled him to weigh in – and it is good for Cabinet ministers to use the resources of their department and those of the Cabinet Office to contribute to a genuinely collective decision. The strength of Cabinet government lies in its ability to draw on departmental expertise and independent legal advice, and in ministers coming briefed to a decision-making meeting of the Cabinet having spoken to a number of experts within the department and some experts from outside, drawing on a knowledge base that enriches and informs the decision-making process. It then has the added advantage of making it more likely that the Cabinet's decision will carry in their political party and in Parliament. Sometimes there is a formalisation of an inner cabinet of seven or eight senior ministers. Cabinet government has, therefore, many forms but in essence the Prime Minister is '*primus inter pares*', not a President. First Margaret Thatcher and then Tony Blair devised techniques to downplay Cabinet decision-making. One big difference was that Margaret Thatcher shared the ideology of her party activists, whereas Tony Blair does not identify with the ideology of his party activists. The other difference is that after the 2001 election, Tony Blair deliberately destroyed the authority and relevance of the Cabinet Office, something Margaret Thatcher never even attempted to do.

Cabinet government as developed during the twentieth century in the UK represents the best way yet found of handling a fusion of the executive and the legislature. Though called a cabinet in the US, it does not govern collectively but serves the President, who is the executive, an arrangement which makes sense where there is a separation of powers between a strong presidential executive and a congressional legislature with real strength. It is difficult but not impossible for the Cabinet in the UK to disown a specific policy of a Prime Minister. Churchill's 1953 attempt at summit diplomacy with the Soviet Union was disowned by the Cabinet. In 1956 Eden, sensing the direction in which the Cabinet was moving, suggested halting the British troops advancing along the Suez Canal. In 1969 the proposed trade union legislation 'In Place of Strife' was abandoned by the Cabinet though Harold Wilson nevertheless remained Prime Minister. Had Margaret Thatcher's rejection of German unification in 1989 continued she might have been challenged by her ministers as it was potentially very damaging to British interests. Fortunately she abandoned this mistaken policy.

Margaret Thatcher for the first few years practised Cabinet government. But even so, by 1982, decisions began to be taken under Margaret Thatcher in No. 10 on the basis of minutes circulated amongst senior Cabinet ministers without meetings, even when there were serious differences. We had a glimpse of this in the Franks report when describing the deployment of HMS *Endurance*. Over the Falklands War, her personal position was on the line. It was understandable that she concentrated decision-making in No. 10 but she also began a process of devaluing the Cabinet. The fact that her new Foreign Secretary, Francis Pym, never had her full confidence helped this process of centralising decisions in No. 10, as did the reality that the Secretary of State for Defence, John Nott, was already a political casualty, having lost command of the House of Commons in the debate on Saturday 3 April. She recruited the recently retired former permanent under-secretary of the Diplomatic Service, Sir Michael Palliser, to help handle the diplomacy of the crisis in No. 10. The Chief of Defence Staff, Admiral of the Fleet Sir Terence Lewin, in effect worked direct to the Prime Minister. A small war cabinet was formed. Few would deny that in conducting a complex fast-moving military operation the whole Cabinet cannot be involved and this procedure worked well over the Falklands crisis, with papers prepared for discussion and the Cabinet and Parliament kept informed.

Margaret Thatcher was, however, determined to take more control of foreign policy. She acquired her first foreign policy adviser in No. 10 at the start of 1983, when Anthony Parsons, previously the UK's permanent representative at the UN, came in to work there three days a week. A defence adviser was also appointed, but interestingly Michael Heseltine refused to co-operate; he forbade his officials to take the adviser's telephone calls and so froze the individual out. The post was soon subsumed under the foreign policy adviser's portfolio[2] and in September Percy Cradock, previously the UK ambassador in China, took over from Anthony Parsons. Cradock initially continued as a deputy under-secretary in the Foreign Office, responsible for the Hong Kong negotiations. From 1985 until he retired in 1992 he combined the job of Prime Minister's adviser with being chairman of the Joint Intelligence Committee with wide responsibilities for British intelligence. The Foreign Office reacted to the new adviser's post by devising a set of self-denying ordinances which the adviser signed.

Problems arose when Charles Powell, authorised to do so by Margaret Thatcher, developed the traditional post of private secretary (foreign affairs) in a way that was far removed from the role of his predecessors' unobtrusive diplomacy and co-operative working with the Foreign Office. During the Westland affair in late 1985–early 1986, Mrs Thatcher's whole style of government began to be seriously questioned. Michael Heseltine after resigning charged her with having destroyed Cabinet government. Even though the Westland helicopter company was being considered by the Cabinet's Economic Committee and not by the Overseas and Defence Committee, the private secretary handling it was Charles Powell and not his nominal superior from the Treasury, Nigel Wicks. According to Geoffrey Howe, who had good reason to resent Powell acting unprecedentedly as gatekeeper for the Foreign Secretary's access to the Prime Minister, Powell was the dominant civil servant in No. 10 and his 'increasingly exclusive role was becoming a matter of serious concern throughout Whitehall as well as in Cabinet'.[3]

An earlier sign that the machinery of government was not working effectively on international affairs came when the heads of government met in Stuttgart on 19 June 1983 for the European Council. They agreed the Solemn Declaration on the European Union as part of relaunching the community. The declaration dealt with everything: economic strategy, the European Monetary System (EMS), economic and monetary union (EMU), economic cohesion, external relations and the developing countries. Completion of the internal market was surprisingly not given great prominence, being included as part of the title 'Development of Community Policies'. By any standard this declaration will be – in the history of the European Community – one of its most significant documents. But it was never seen as such at the time by the UK, whether in government, Parliament or the press.

The declaration was described in the half-yearly report to Parliament on developments in the European Community as the 'Genscher/ Colombo Declaration', saying it was 'not a legal instrument and involves no Treaty amendments or increases in the powers of the institutions'. How wrong that proved to be. That declaration paved the way for much more than just the single market: for far more extensive use of qualified majority voting, and for the claim that a single market needs a single currency, which I believe is a false claim.

The declaration, by bringing together the EMS and EMU, disguised the fact that they were different conceptual designs. The EMS is a technical way, albeit flawed, as we in the UK saw in 1992, of trying to achieve monetary stability, whereas EMU is first and foremost a political structure involving abandoning UK control of interest rates and the government and Parliament no longer being able to set inflation and unemployment targets; it is done through locking national currencies together and then merging them into one currency. Not enough attention was given throughout the 1980s in the UK to the nature of the political agenda that lay behind EMU. Eventually this was dealt with in a Maastricht Treaty opt-out by Prime Minister John Major. John Major, to his credit, did return some power to the Foreign Secretary, Douglas Hurd; also the post of foreign policy adviser lapsed.

One powerful political figure who has never blurred the distinction between EMS and EMU is Nigel Lawson. Even as financial secretary in 1981, while pretty open minded about joining the Exchange Rate Mechanism (ERM) he was adamantly against EMU. In his auto-biography,[4] he explains how both he and Geoffrey Howe tried in 1985 to join the ERM. The Prime Minister, however, simply vetoed ERM entry by saying: 'If you join the EMS, you will have to do so without me.' An implicit veto is part of a Prime Minister's legitimate authority. Lawson and Howe were not willing to risk all by asking the Cabinet to endorse ERM entry. But in effect by then Cabinet government had been gravely weakened, as the Westland affair confirmed.

After ignoring Nigel Lawson's views on the ERM Mrs Thatcher was in no mood, a few weeks later, to treat seriously his specific objections to making any new treaty commitments in what was to become the Single Act covering European monetary union prior to the meeting of the European Council in Luxembourg in December 1985. Lawson sent her two memos, one, dated 14 November, saying that 'the inclusion of EMU as a treaty objective would be a political commitment going well beyond previous references to EMU, which have been non-binding European Council resolutions or solemn declarations'.[5] Again on 28 November he minuted her:

There should be no reference in the treaty to EMU, since this – which implies progress towards a common currency and a common central bank – would be no more credible to outside opinion than the commitments entered into in 1971 and 1972 and is, in any case, politically unacceptable to the UK.[6]

Margaret Thatcher in her memoirs recalls some of Nigel Lawson's warnings but claims that the formula she accepted, which added to the phrase 'economic and monetary union', provided an important gloss by describing it as 'co-operation in economic and monetary policy' and that this signalled the limits the Act placed on it.[7] She thought she had surrendered no important British interest but this was emphatically not the case.

It is very bizarre and a reflection on the considerable limitations of unrestrained prime ministerial decision-making that even with Charles Powell advising her, who like her was always against EMU, she personally, albeit by default, conceded the objective of EMU in the community. It cannot be respectably argued that this was the price for achieving her principal objective, the single market, or, as it was then termed, the internal market, for this was already agreed within the community and all ready to be put in place. Nevertheless a new major and unjustifiable concession over monetary union was extracted from a Prime Minister who was utterly opposed to the very principle of monetary union. It was also done against the advice of her Chancellor of the Exchequer and without substantive discussion in Cabinet. This could only have happened within the framework within which European policies are developed, with far less accountability to the Cabinet and Parliament than other areas of government decision-making.

The 1985 EMU wording gave the newly reappointed President of the European Commission, Jacques Delors, the pre-legislative authority he wanted to bring about a single European currency. Margaret Thatcher's surprising concession was then compounded at the European Council in Hanover in June 1988 by her agreeing to establish a committee of the community's central bank governors in their personal capacities, to be chaired by Jacques Delors. When challenged in the House of Commons about this new committee, Margaret Thatcher merely reiterated:

> With regard to the European Central Bank, we have taken part in the Single European Act, which went through the House and which said that we would make progressive steps to the realisation of monetary union, and we have set up a group to consider that. Monetary union would be the first step, but progress towards it would not necessarily involve a single currency or a European Central Bank.

If even an inner cabinet had operated in 1985 it would have been easier for Treasury objections, like Lawson's, to be heard.

Over the Maastricht negotiations in 1991 under John Major as Prime Minister, other departmental ministers' views were taken into account, particularly those of Michael Howard. Under Harold Wilson in the run-up to the 1975 referendum the Cabinet was involved through Wilson and the Foreign Secretary, James Callaghan. They masterminded the so-called renegotiations and swung the 'yes' vote in the referendum. Under James Callaghan in 1977 the Cabinet established the all-important enlargement priority as the best counter to federalism on a paper the Prime Minister asked me, as Foreign Secretary, to write for a political Cabinet with no officials present.[8] Progressive enlargement became thereafter a key UK priority under all governments for checking integration. The first priority in 1977 was to ensure that Portugal and Spain came into the community in addition to Greece, enlarging from nine members to twelve. Then twelve became fifteen, then twenty-five, and from January 2007 the EU has twenty-seven member states, with Romania and Bulgaria. The Cabinet were involved in 1978–9 under Callaghan in the decision to join the EMS but to stay out of the ERM. Under John Major in 1991 the Cabinet was fully involved in demanding two opt-outs for the UK, on joining the euro and the social chapter.

The role of Prime Minister does not, however, exist in isolation. It has had to adapt to changed patterns both at home and abroad. From 1992 to 1995, as the EU negotiator in the Balkans, I saw the structure of UK government as it had evolved since I was Foreign Secretary in 1977–9. I was made virtually an honorary member of the European Council of Foreign Ministers and given access to Foreign Office telegrams and saw many matters referred to No. 10 which in my day I would have settled within the department. I well understood why this was so, for there had been a clear trend for Prime Ministers to be sucked into decisions over the common foreign and security policy (CFSP), through ever more meetings and what are now the quarterly meetings of the European Council. Also more heads of government travel to London, more issues cross over into more departments. But when all that is admitted, it does not mean that Cabinet government has to be abandoned. In fact, it becomes more important to have prior Cabinet discussion, for when a Prime Minister states a policy the press ensure that it is then virtually set in concrete. Also, in fairness to Tony Blair, NATO's involvement in the war in Kosovo in 1999 and the events of 11 September 2001 in the United States, as well as the global threat of Al-Qaeda, the removal of the Taliban government in Afghanistan and the invasion of Iraq, were all events which would have brought any incumbent in No. 10 more and more into a dialogue with other heads of government, with greater involvement in decision-making on international affairs. Yet these complex issues in many ways should have made Tony Blair readier to draw on a wider range of experience than his own. Unfortunately he had just before 9/11 chosen to centralise decision-making on a permanent basis in No 10 and involve the FCO and Ministry of Defence even less.

In Tony Blair's first term his method of working was fairly close to that of Margaret Thatcher. Cabinet government was set to one side, power was sucked into No. 10, but by and large he was working with the same institutional structures, including the key departments. In 2001 after the general election he made the most sweeping changes ever made in the conduct of UK foreign and security policy. He brought the European Unit from the Cabinet Office, where under earlier governments it had worked co-ordinating departmental responsibilities, into No. 10 as a new European Secretariat and created a new Overseas and Defence Secretariat, again in No. 10, drawing from some of the Cabinet Office functions previously supervised by the Cabinet Secretary. The secretariats were headed up by two high-flying permanent under-secretaries – Stephen Wall and David Manning – coming from being the UK's permanent representatives to the EU and NATO. Both were ideally qualified for each job, both at the peak of their careers and both capable of working all hours of the day and night and backed by a small staff. Despite both secretariats doing all they could to involve the Foreign Office and the Defence Ministry, the structure within which they worked could not do anything else but create a personal decision-making point around the Prime Minister. However hard the secretariats strove to involve that wider expertise that existed in the three large departments of Foreign, Defence and Overseas Development, the structure within which they worked concentrated advice, power and executive command in the person of Tony Blair. This was no accident, for he designed it to do so. The first challenge facing this new structure was the integrationists' wish to reopen the Nice Treaty and have yet another intergovernmental conference.

Sadly, we saw the results in the Constitutional Treaty, when Tony Blair made many of the same mistakes that Margaret Thatcher made over the Single Act. The loose way in which the convention set up to draft the treaty was established at Laeken should have been challenged. Accepting the use of the convention procedure, even though it had already produced the dangerously diffuse Charter of Fundamental Rights, was a mistake. There was no need to concede so soon that there would have to be a constitution and UK ministers repeatedly misjudged the momentum for an all-enveloping constitution that the convention was building up.

Fortunately the Constitutional Treaty was rejected by the French and the Dutch. The UK has not yet seen the potential dangers lurking in that text. The UK has drifted into accepting positions which will come back to haunt us through a saga of incompetence. First Keith Vaz and then Peter Hain showed their inexperience as ministers for Europe; Vaz described the Declaration of Fundamental Rights as being of no more significance than the *Beano* and Hain described the Constitutional Treaty as being merely a 'tidying-up exercise'. Both were facile observations and there were many such similar comments. When France and Germany saw the convention gaining in influence they moved promptly to increase their representation to that of their Foreign Ministers, who obtained much of what they wanted. The Foreign Secretary, Jack Straw, should have joined the negotiations then. He is good on detail and a lawyer, as I know well, for he worked as a political adviser for Peter Shore, whose mastery of European matters I used to encounter regularly when I chaired the European Cabinet Committee. The reason why Straw was not involved until after the treaty was tabled by Giscard d'Estaing was that having Hain there ensured Prime Ministerial control. To achieve the Prime Minister's personal priority for a president of the European Council, the UK expended far too much negotiating capital. Also Tony Blair put too much reliance in the prior negotiating of UK representation on the convention in having a retired former permanent under-secretary for the Diplomatic Service, Sir John Kerr, as the head of its secretariat. John Kerr's loyalty and brilliant mind had to primarily serve the convention's president, Giscard d'Estaing, not the UK. After one term as French President Giscard had become a member of the European Parliament and, along with a number of centrist French politicians, an integrationist, though, being French, with a limited place still for sovereign governments. The UK inexplicably felt it necessary to accept that the intergovernmental pillared structure of Maastricht should be abandoned. The UK also agreed damaging wording on defence: namely that, unlike in the existing Nice Treaty, where it states that a common European defence policy *might* occur, the wording was changed to '*will* occur'. This represented a profound change, based in the view of some states on the French definition of common defence, because it in effect excludes the primary role of NATO. The British government also abandoned their previous insistence in the Nice Treaty that the EU would not be able to establish structured co-operation within the framework of enhanced co-operation 'in matters having military and defence implications'.

The Chirac–Blair St Malo agreement over defence in December 1998, further compounded by the disarray in the EU in the run-up to Nice, caused considerable anxiety in NATO for some years. Fortunately this looked as if it might have been resolved by the EU–NATO–Berlin-plus negotiations. Yet hardly was the ink dry on this before the Constitutional Treaty called common defence once again into question. France, Germany, Belgium and Luxembourg were being offered that which they were much derided for advocating a few months before – a separate European common defence policy. 'Structured co-operation' on defence was in the treaty text, and it is explicitly defined as the same as enhanced co-operation. On 11 December 2000 Tony Blair in a statement to the House of Commons after the Nice negotiations actually praised the exclusion of defence from enhanced co-operation as 'another key British objective'. Yet the Prime Minister went to Berlin on 20 September 2003 and conceded structured defence co-operation while Parliament was not sitting and without making any formal public announcement. This was not even parliamentary government, let alone Cabinet government.

The Constitutional Treaty also asked the UK to accept the new title of a Union Minister for Foreign Affairs, who was also to be a vice-president of the Commission. So much for CFSP being purely inter-governmental. This first ever advocacy of the name 'Minister' in any EU document is a clear attempt to present the EU as a government. The British government, we were told, was unhappy with this, yet irresolute when it came to refusing to accept the term 'Minister' in the text.

The lesson of all this is that the community method can only be checked and on occasions defeated with intellectual rigour and by involving the whole range of skills available to the UK government through the Cabinet Office. That combination of skills was effectively deployed over the Maastricht Treaty negotiations with the creation of the pillared treaty structure and its two intergovernmental pillars. The pillared structure was an essential safeguard for intergovernmentalism yet it was washed away in the treaty text by a mixture of inattention to detail in the convention and much political wishful thinking by Tony Blair. His obsession was with creating a new institutional paid post of President of the European Council. Blair always denied that he would be a candidate but those close to his decision-making believed that at some stages he saw this as a job to go to after he stepped down as Prime Minister. It was seized on after initial suspicion by the integrationists as a mechanism for a future 'big bang' integration. The final wording about this post allowed in the legal view of the Dutch government for it to be 'double-hatted' with that of the President of the Commission. This could have meant a real President of Europe emerging through a qualified majority on the European Council and subject only to a possible appeal to the European Court of Justice on the UK interpretation that double-hatting was ruled out.

Without firm moorings any EU negotiating position is swept away by winds and tides of the integrationists' long-term goals. It is a characteristic of personalised decision-making that it deals best with broad concepts, but the community method progresses through detailed legalistic drafting which pushes integration by nuance and sleight of hand. The eventual Constitutional Treaty showed time and again how British government positions advanced in the early stages had been abandoned, each perhaps understandable on their own, but cumulatively the effect was to make the treaty a vehicle on which the integrationists could build.

Experience indicates that the integrationists' objectives have been achieved in the community and still are being achieved in the European Union most frequently when the UK's European decision-making is concentrated with the Prime Minister in No. 10, whether it was Margaret Thatcher or now Tony Blair. Under this process, Prime

Ministers acquiesce in committees or conventions being established by the European Council often without full consultation with the Cabinet. When these reports are then received the next step is that advisers argue that there is no danger of imminent action since it is only an agreement in principle, and does not call for specific action. It is then Prime Ministers who agree in principle in the Council, sometimes but not always following full Cabinet discussion; in the late-night negotiations it tends to be forgotten that the principle is then included in all future statements or declarations of objectives. Then incorporation of the principle in the wording for a suggested treaty comes into a Commission first draft, albeit tentative, and, it develops then a semi-official status. It gains support amongst member states, perhaps with a UK reservation, until at an IGC to prevent it becoming binding legislation a Prime Minister has to be ready to hold out and veto the wording. If a Prime Minister is ready to veto they risk the charge of being unnecessarily provocative from their fellow heads of government and they wonder how many vetos they can use. The argument is then made that one cannot fight on too many fronts at the same time, one has to prioritise. Margaret Thatcher talked a lot about using the veto but allowed the big issue of EMU to progress. In the case of Tony Blair, because of his criticism of John Major using the veto, one senses that he has been peculiarly reluctant to use the veto. This process was speeded up by the convention and the Constitutional Treaty, fatally flawed, with unacknowledged far-reaching consequences. Only a referendum ensured the French and the Dutch rejections. Only very reluctantly after a public campaign was a referendum promised for the UK. The first test of the new European secretariat inside No. 10 was therefore an unmitigated failure. But there are few, if any, signs that Tony Blair or his successor has recognised this reality.

A problem uniquely facing Tony Blair was that he needed to dominate foreign and security policy because he very clearly did not dominate economic and fiscal policy. Almost all the criticism of 'President' Blair falls at the first fence for he allowed Gordon Brown a decision-making power which went far beyond that conceded by any other post-war Prime Minister to their Chancellor of the Exchequer, whether Attlee to Cripps, Churchill to Butler, Wilson to Jenkins, Callaghan to Healey, Thatcher to Lawson or Major to Clarke. As a consequence we have had two huge areas of policy largely outside the normal Cabinet machinery: one economic policy controlled by the Chancellor from the Treasury, one overseas policy controlled by the Prime Minister from No. 10.

Whereas in my day the Foreign Office was also responsible for overseas development, that was made a separate ministry again in 1997 by Tony Blair, repeating the mistake Wilson made from 1964 to 1970. This has also served not only to diminish the role of the Foreign Secretary but allowed the Prime Minister to assume an oversight function of development policies too and with the Commission on Africa it ensured he built up specific expertise again within No. 10. Yet how was it possible to appoint the discredited Ethiopian head of government to that commission? How was it thought credible to avoid serious discussion of Zimbabwe in the commission report?

For a short while, in 2001 and 2002, it looked as if this new centralisation of foreign and defence policy in No. 10 was succeeding. Blair and Bush were in constant communication and if Geoff Hoon and Jack Straw featured far less than Donald Rumsfeld and Colin Powell over Iraq, few cared as long as it worked. Blair's honeymoon period from 1997 to 2003, like Thatcher's from 1982 to 1988, looked as if it would last. But it has not lasted. Hubris was followed by nemesis for Thatcher. So hubris for Blair was followed by nemesis over the incompetent handling of the aftermath of the invasion of Iraq in 2003.

The biggest foreign and security policy failure in the UK prior to Iraq had been Suez, when Eden as Prime Minister brought the canal into No. 10 with disastrous consequences. We have had three tests of Tony Blair's new No. 10 secretariat and his style of personal diplomacy and 'sofa government'. On Iraq, Afghanistan and the EU constitution the Prime Minister has not been able to carry the broad consent of the

British public. Bipartisan consent is normally given for international policies. Blair had the support of the Conservatives over Iraq and Afghanistan, though not on the Constitutional Treaty. The absence of bipartisan support does not of itself make government policies wrong, but it is troubling for any democrat and it should make for a questioning of the way in which the government is making its decisions.

On the Iraq war I supported the invasion and still support it. I did so primarily because I believed that once the US President was ready to again invade Iraq, this time with the specific purpose of toppling Saddam Hussein, it was a British interest, as in 1991, to be there fighting alongside US troops. The Hutton inquiry and the Butler report exonerated the Prime Minister from deliberately lying about intelligence matters. Nevertheless it is impossible to believe that Sir Anthony Duff, Sir Percy Cradock or Dame Pauline Neville-Jones, to name but three former heads of the Joint Intelligence Committee, with whom I have worked, would ever have conducted themselves as John Scarlett, now head of MI6, did with Jonathan Powell and Alastair Campbell over the intelligence assessments on Iraqi weapons of mass destruction. The other so-called 'dodgy' dossier for which Alastair Campbell has already apologised left our joint intelligence services a laughing stock. Amongst the reasons for these failures was the 'matey', corner-cutting, somewhat shambolic, structure of No. 10's defence and security decision-making, which was revealed in the Hutton inquiry public hearings. I am content to accept that there was no deliberate lying to Parliament by ministers, the government generally or MI6. But it stretches common sense to deny that there was not persistent manipulation and exaggeration of the intelligence, deliberately losing the nuances and doubts that come with most intelligence reporting.

I do not pretend, however, that I feel personally misled by Tony Blair over what he said over weapons of mass destruction and I too have been surprised that none have been found. Nevertheless, millions of British citizens do feel deceived. Ever since Saddam Hussein attacked the Kurds and the Marsh Arabs after the ceasefire in 1991, I felt it was desirable to topple Saddam Hussein from power for the good of the whole Middle East region. I have argued the justification for military action in terms of the UN Charter and in Saddam Hussein's flagrant disregard of the many UN ceasefire resolutions from 1991 onwards. It is in the interests of everyone who wants to avoid bloodshed to uphold the concept of negotiated ceasefires and not reach a state of international cynicism over the authority of the UN such that wars can only be ended by unconditional surrender with consequentially much greater loss of life.

Over Iraq it is not my purpose to carp but to pose relevant questions. The Cabinet discussed Iraq fairly frequently but as we have seen superficially. There was no formal Cabinet subcommittee or Cabinet paper circulated even though some were prepared. The Foreign Office, the Ministry of Defence and the Ministry of Overseas Development [*sic*] were nowhere near as deeply involved in 2002–3 as they had been in 1990–1. In part this seems to be why the UK was not able to plan itself for the war's aftermath more effectively or to take British ideas to America for collective discussion. We cannot just blame the US administration. While Basra has, it appears, been somewhat better handled than Baghdad, it was a much easier city to influence. Nevertheless there have still been major deficiencies in our own UK post-war area of responsibility. In the first Gulf War of 1990–1, to force the Iraqis out of Kuwait our co-operation with the US military was based on component commanders and a joint force commander who had considerable influence. We knew we were going to fight for months ahead and we planned accordingly in good time. Even so there were failures over the ceasefire terms and for what Saddam Hussein was able to do to the Kurds and Marsh Arabs. In the 2003 Iraq war we deployed military forces late and only had contingent commanders and a national contingent commander. Did this mean we were so fully integrated with the American lead operation that we lost a crucial measure of independence? Why was an airman our senior officer in the US commander's HQ when it was obvious the Iraqi planes would be taken out and we knew from experience in Afghanistan that the same US commanding general's strong point was not nation-building? Would it not have been wiser to safeguard the post-war period by having an officer from the UK with experience of nation-building?

Lord Franks conducted an inquiry into the Falklands War. Probably the reason we had the inquiry was that the decision to hold it was conceded at a time of Margaret Thatcher's maximum political weakness – during, not after, the Argentinean occupation. Had a sufficient number of Labour MPs voted for an inquiry on Iraq in 2006, it would have focused on intelligence before the invasion and examined the competence of the Prime Minister and how much his mistakes related back to the way the Iraqi war was run by the Overseas and Defence Secretariat within No. 10.

The initial military campaign was very successful and the US in particular maintained political momentum, having gone to Congress for authorisation in the autumn of 2002. Waiting as the UK did for parliamentary approval in 2003 reduced our influence on US planning for the aftermath of the invasion. This was, we know, far too Pentagon dominated in the US. Post-war planning in the UK was hampered by politicians keeping their fingers crossed that there would not be a war. The Prime Minister was, however, warned in a meeting on 23 July 2002 by Sir Richard Dearlove, then the head of MI6, following a visit to Washington, that he and the Chiefs of Defence Staff were not satisfied about the state of post-war planning. The chiefs were continuing to ask lots of questions, including what the consequences were if Saddam used WMD on day one or if Baghdad did not collapse and urban war fighting began.

An inquiry into the Prime Minister's handling of Iraq would ask many questions:

- What happened about UK planning for the aftermath in the light of Dearlove's warning?
- Did the UK never anticipate that Saddam Hussein might stage a guerrilla war after defeat?

- What was the basis for the belief that formed Iraqi military units would come across to the coalition?

- Why was so little done to stop Iraqi units disbanding in the wake of the invasion, or to protect ammunition dumps?

- Most of the Iraqi armed forces just disappeared with their weapons. Why were those left in the Iraqi army so unwisely and precipitately allowed to disband?

- Was the UK consulted about the formal disbandment by US Ambassador Bremer? Bremer also claims to have supported a far larger force to stabilise Iraq in the aftermath of the invasion. Why did the Prime Minister, through 2003 and especially in November 2004, not accept Colin Powell's advice given to him and President Bush in the White House to increase force levels?

- Ambassador John Sawers, as an emergency temporary appointment from being ambassador in Cairo, did a fine job on the ground in Iraq after the initial invasion, as did Jeremy Greenstock, who followed him. Yet why was there no one earmarked for this role months before the invasion to go into Iraq, along with General Tim Cross, who was under General Jay Garner?

- Why did we not put in a very senior political or diplomatic figure, albeit perhaps temporarily, into Washington once the ambassador, Christopher Meyer, felt he had to return to the UK and David Manning could not be spared from No. 10 because of the impending war? This was no time to be represented by a deputy in Washington, even though a very able one. This was particularly so given the known differences between Colin Powell's State Department and Donald Rumsfeld's Pentagon about post-war reconstruction.

The answer to many of these questions lies in No. 10's belief that they and they alone could handle all these issues, drawing, when they wanted to, on military and intelligence advisers. Christopher Meyer has written that between 9 September 2001 and his retirement as ambassador to Washington in February 2003, the period which also coincided with the newly introduced Overseas and Defence Secretariat inside No. 10, he did not have a single substantive policy discussion on the secure phone with the Foreign Office.[9] His frequent substantive dialogue was directly with No. 10. It is hard to avoid the judgement that there has never been a previous war when the British Foreign Office counted for less.

An Iraq inquiry would question the personalised nature of the Prime Minister's diplomacy. Why, for all the Prime Minister's bilateral, trilateral and multilateral meetings with Jacques Chirac and Gerhard Schröder, did he fail to pick up on a French offer to live with action under the first resolution, provided the second resolution was dropped? Were there any warnings from the Foreign Office about going for a second resolution and losing the vote in the Security Council? Tony Blair wanted the second resolution but the Americans had no intention of seeking a second resolution. They were content with Resolution 1441, passed unanimously by the Security Council in November. Risking a rebuff by then in the UN Security Council was judged too great a gamble, particularly after Bush had rightly been persuaded by Blair to go for and win the first vote in the Security Council. The US State Department under Colin Powell did not believe in a second resolution. Why did Tony Blair believe he could avoid a veto and win around enough small countries to have the necessary nine votes on the Security Council? Did Tony Blair only consult our ambassador at the UN? What was the view of the UN Department inside the FCO? We already had all the authority we needed from past UN resolutions and eventually relied on this justification for the attack when we were forced to withdraw the second resolution. The loss of moral authority before the war had started in defying a majority on the Security Council was very damaging.

One has to go back to Suez for a parallel where a Prime Minister on his own drives through such a flawed plan. The problems of Iraq we now face in 2007 are, I hope, still resolvable. The Iraqi police and army are being rebuilt. They may be able to impact more on the deteriorating security situation, with the US and UK military acting as reinforcing rapid reaction forces based outside the cities and less visible on the streets. The restoration of public services has been slow and Iraqi oil production has taken far too long to pick up. Iraq needs more genuinely international help from Syria, Turkey and possibly Iran, avoiding the impression of the US attempting to take all the decisions about Iraq's future stability.

The initial US–UK military success has been followed by a very serious rebuff but artificial deadlines will end in scuttle. There are deep political questions as to why UK diplomacy failed so miserably in the UN, truly worrying questions about how UK intelligence over uranium from Niger to Iraq and the alleged 45-minute warning of an Iraqi missile launch were handled politically. Why were the borders with Iran and Syria left so open for Al-Qaeda to infiltrate?

We urgently need an authoritative independent review in the UK, and preferably on both sides of the Atlantic, about force levels. Above all, we need new leadership. Rumsfeld has gone. Blair's mistake has been to hang on too long. The Butler report said of Tony Blair's decision-making: 'We are concerned that the informality and circumscribed character of the government's procedures . . . risks reducing the scope for informed collective political judgement.'

No one can credibly argue that the two new No. 10 secretariats, one covering Europe, the other Iraq and Afghanistan, have delivered. They failed not because they were not ably staffed but because their very existence only fed the Prime Minister's illusion that all these complex European and foreign policy issues could be handled by himself. His personal diplomacy, frequently flying around for much-publicised talks on Christian-name terms with heads of government that were not properly prepared and just used as the vehicle for his own views, has been shown to have serious limitations. The brighter the people involved in the secretariats the longer the illusion was able to be maintained that this degree of centralised decision-making could succeed. The illusion has been shattered by not just UK but European public opinion over the European constitution and by the extent of the public disillusionment over the conduct of the aftermath of the Iraq and Afghanistan wars.

I unashamedly champion the return of the *ancien régime* of Cabinet government in the UK's national interest. Tony Blair has failed to use his remaining time in office to fashion a collective structure that we all can trust to make sensible decisions. There is no longer any valid justification for his experimental structure. It has been a disaster on the ground and has not managed to establish consent at home. This government has now to re-establish consent for the future development of the European Union and for military intervention. The failure to convince covers people who had different views on the desirability of a European constitution and different views on the advisability of invading Iraq.

It is not just a matter of the next Prime Minister forgoing spin or changing the Blair style. This top-down approach does not work. The substance of governmental policy needs redesigning and reinforcing by drawing on a wider pool of talent within departments and learning from experienced expert opinion within Cabinet and outside government. An inquiry on Iraq and Afghanistan, like the Dardanelles Commission, would draw important lessons for a structure of Cabinet collective decision-making capable of carrying the full-hearted consent of the British people for its policies.

The euro for the UK is now a very distant prospect. Tony Blair, in search of a legacy, must be prevented from smuggling in, via the back door, aspects of the ill-fated and poorly thought through constitution. A bringing together of the roles of Javier Solana, the EU Foreign Policy Representative, and the EU Commissioner for External Affairs can make sense but that does not mean creating a 'minister'. We must reject the pretence that the EU is a government. For somewhat different reasons the UK must also veto creating a new institution with a 'President' of the European Council who is not a serving elected head of government. Either of these changes must necessitate a referendum in the UK.

One change is vital. The present structure of personal power that dominates Whitehall must be changed. Candidates for replacing Tony Blair as Prime Minister should be urged to pledge to end his two new international secretariats in No. 10 and share more power with the Cabinet. If his successor proves to be Gordon Brown he must accept that he cannot exercise the same personal hold over Treasury policy from No. 10, let alone also over the Foreign Office and the Ministry of Defence, if he wants to be a good Prime Minister. The personal fiefdoms of these two able politicians, largely unanswerable to the Cabinet, may have helped the inexperienced New Labour government establish itself, but now there are emerging other serious players in the Cabinet. The Conservative Party is also becoming a credible opposition party. The government's competence, coherence and credibility at home and abroad is now widely questioned and it is urgent that personal fiefdoms be replaced with real Cabinet government under a new Prime Minister.

The Rt Hon. the Lord Carrington
KG GCMG CH MC

Foreign Secretary May 1979–April 1982

'The continuing problems'

Based on a lecture given at the London School of Economics
and Political Science, 16 October 2003

I note with interest the title of David Owen's chapter, 'The Ever-Growing Dominance of No. 10 in British Diplomacy since 5 April 1982'. And note particularly the date which he maintains No. 10 took over foreign policy. This was the day I resigned as Foreign Secretary. It will be interesting to read how my successors deal with the implications of that on their independence.

I had an experience on the other side of the fence at one time. I was rather unexpectedly parachuted, many years ago, to be high commissioner in Australia, and the Foreign Office in London at that time didn't think it worthwhile to airmail the dispatches of European ambassadors to Canberra; they came by sea. I remember reading one in 1958 which went something like this: I spent a dismal Sunday talking to a sad, lonely, old man who knew that never again would he have the opportunity to lead his country and follow his destiny. When I read it, General de Gaulle had been back in power for three months. It taught me to be very careful of making any predictions in my dispatches and later on, as Secretary of State, to be as careful in believing the predictions of others.

I entitled this chapter 'The Continuing Problems'. Some people may think that an incoming Foreign Secretary has the world at his feet but in reality he has to deal with events as he finds them. It would be splendid if a Foreign Secretary could start his tenure with a clean sheet – a world with no wars, no long-standing disagreements, all quarrels and differences resolved. He or she could announce with a flourish that henceforward British foreign policy would start afresh. New initiatives, which, as a prospective Foreign Secretary, he had prepared during the years of opposition, initiatives which would transform Britain's standing in the world and, of course, his prospects as well. Alas, it's not like that!

An incoming Foreign Secretary has to deal with all the problems which faced his predecessor, some of them long-standing and seemingly impossible to resolve. He or she has to address the divisions in his own party, which are usually just as deep as those between the two parties. For example, the position of Britain in Europe is as controversial in the two parties as it is between them. Iraq is another issue which divides parties as it does the country. But on the whole, foreign policy has been bipartisan and that is not particularly surprising. The Foreign Secretary is there to look after Britain's interests and those are not usually a matter of party politics. When I became Foreign Secretary, the world was still divided between East and West. The Cold War, though not at its height, was still by far the most important issue in foreign policy. The threat to our way of life seemed very real and our support for the Atlantic alliance was crucial.

Surprised though I was as an hereditary peer to become Foreign Secretary, I was not astonished to find so many other issues which were fairly familiar and which occupied a great deal of my time. I have called them 'the continuing problems'. The three I have chosen will be very familiar, but there may possibly be some lessons to be learnt from them and our handling of them. Two of them were on my desk in 1979: Zimbabwe and the Falklands. The third is Yugoslavia, with which I became involved some years later.

The first was the perennial problem of Rhodesia/Zimbabwe. Over the years, successive British governments had tried to solve what had become an increasingly difficult and dangerous problem. In 1979 the position had become more acute. An inordinate amount of the Foreign Office's time was occupied with the Rhodesian problem and it was spilling over into relations with the European Union [sic], the United States, whose President at the time was President Carter, and the whole of the Commonwealth.

There had been an election in which Bishop Muzorewa, supported by the white Rhodesians, had won an overwhelming victory. The trouble was that neither Joshua Nkomo's party nor Robert Mugabe's party had taken part in the election and the result was clearly not representative of the broad spectrum of opinion in the country. Awkwardly, the government was faced with a semi-pledge that if Lord Boyd, who was asked to investigate the election, said that the election was fair, there might be recognition of that regime. He did so and, indeed, so far as African elections go, it was fairly conducted. The difficulty that faced us was not just that the two main opposition parties had not been involved but that, with the exception of South Africa, no other country would recognise the Muzorewa regime. The consequences of this threatened to be very serious. President Carter's government made it clear where they stood, as indeed did the European Union: they were wholly opposed to recognising Muzorewa.

There was a groundswell of opinion in the Commonwealth, not just that the Muzorewa regime was unacceptable and undemocratic, but that the consequences for the Commonwealth as a whole and Britain's part in it might lead to dissolution and/or sanctions. An added difficulty, from my point of view, was that this was one of the issues which did not divide the Labour Party, but certainly divided the Conservative Party. A substantial body of opinion on the right of the party believed not only that the Muzorewa regime should be recognised, but that black majority rule which, incidentally, all parties were committed to, would be a disaster and a betrayal of the whites. The erstwhile Suez Group was belligerently opposed to a settlement on those lines. There was a substantial body of opinion in the Conservative Party in favour of Ian Smith. We felt therefore that it was essential to try, yet again, to come to an agreement with the parties involved. The forthcoming Commonwealth heads of government meeting seemed the appropriate forum to try and arrange a conference in London, as a last attempt to settle the problem.

After a shaky start, we were successful and the Lancaster House conference took place later in the year. This, in itself, was perhaps one of the most important lessons to be drawn. Once all parties had agreed to attend and take part, it was much more difficult for them to walk out. More particularly since the African delegations knew that the only possible alternative to an agreed solution was recognition of the Muzorewa regime, which of course was wholly unacceptable to them.

This didn't mean, however, that the bargaining and the histrionics and the prevarications were any less. One factor in its eventual success was the decision to exclude from the conference and its building all those not directly involved and, in particular, those Presidents close to the parties involved. The problem was Zimbabwe, an internal affair.

This caused much indignation, particularly on the part of President Nyerere,[1] but was absolutely right. For me, as chairman, it was a fairly disagreeable few months, lightened sometimes by a touch of humour. When I had to announce that we were proposing to send a British governor to resume legitimacy which unilateral independence had broken, it was hardly going to be popular with anyone in the room. Blacks and whites regarded a return to colonial rule as outrageous.

When I announced that Christopher Soames, who had gallantly accepted the poisoned chalice, was to leave and take up his position of governor, there was a stunned silence, which lasted for what seemed to me to be a very long time. Finally, Joshua Nkomo put up his hand and said very seriously: 'Will he have plumes and a horse?' God bless the shade of Joshua Nkomo!

In the event we got an agreement and an election which, broadly speaking, was as fair and as representative as an election of that kind is likely to be. Subsequent events are, I am afraid, only too well known to all of us, but it is fair to say that for the first fifteen years of independence, Robert Mugabe behaved with a certain magnanimity and with a realisation that the whites in Zimbabwe were vital in the success of the economy. He had in Tanzania and Mozambique seen the economic consequences of expelling the white community. It was only when things started to go wrong, largely due to economic mismanagement, that he decided to play the racist card and, alas, the welfare of Zimbabwe, its people and its economy became less important than the welfare and survival of President Mugabe. Shameful, disgraceful and inhuman, and not yet over.

But that was all in the future and it is interesting to speculate as to why the Lancaster House conference was successful when other attempts had failed. I think the answer is quite simple. For one reason or another, all parties concerned wanted a settlement. The Smith government was in real difficulty: manpower and the economy was stretched to the limit, as so many were fighting against the Patriotic Front that the economy was in danger of collapse. After a period of fifteen years, sanctions were beginning to bite. Moreover, the South African government, whose help was absolutely vital to the Smith government, were becoming less and less inclined to bail them out. It was in the interests of both the white Rhodesians and the South African government that a settlement should be reached.

In so far as Joshua Nkomo and his party were concerned, Nkomo, who was really the father of the Patriotic Front, was becoming increasingly sidelined by Mugabe and was getting on in years, wanted to be President of the new republic and felt that time was not on his side, since Mugabe was becoming increasingly the dominant partner. President Kenneth Kaunda of Zambia, on whose territory most of Nkomo's forces were based, was becoming more and more restive at the problems Nkomo was causing him.

Mugabe, on the other hand, had no such problems. His troops were doing the fighting; he believed that he was winning and that it was only a matter of time before he won the overall victory. But his supporters in the shape of President Julius Nyerere in Tanzania and President Samora Moisés Machel of Mozambique were becoming increasingly worried about the lack of food which the Zimbabweans exported to their countries and which, as a result of the war, had diminished to nothing, and of course the disruption the fighting caused. They were putting pressure on Mugabe to come to the conference and try for a negotiated settlement. So it was for a variety of reasons that all the parties concerned were prepared for a conference. Of course, all of them thought that in the end their own particular interests would emerge triumphant and though it may not have turned out like that, it became increasingly difficult for them to leave the conference table.

What are the lessons to be learnt from that? Whatever the problems of a particular dispute, we must always try, however difficult, to find a solution, even in the most unpromising circumstances. Realistically, no solutions are going to be found unless all the participants are willing to compromise, need a solution or are in the position of having their arm twisted to accept a compromise. We see that only too clearly in Palestine and Israel and also in Northern Ireland. But it is equally important to see the moment when the settlement is possible and not let the opportunity go by.

The second problem with which I was concerned as Foreign Secretary was that of the Falklands. You will need no reminding of the issues involved. The islands had been a matter of dispute between Britain and Argentina over a great many years. There had been desultory negotiations, but no prospect of agreement. The Argentineans claimed the islands to be Argentinean territory and we maintained, equally vigorously, that they were British.

Over several years leading up to 1979, there had been a gradual escalation by the Argentineans of their claim to the islands and fruitless negotiations had taken place. I came to the conclusion that if we were to avoid serious trouble, it was necessary for us to try, yet again, to negotiate some kind of settlement. The difficulty was to find a negotiating position which would be acceptable in this country and at the same time likely to appeal to the Argentineans. I thought that if we made no signs of being prepared to negotiate or of making any proposals, the Argentineans, under a volatile dictatorship, might well use it as an excuse for taking action. Not necessarily military action, but action in the United Nations, in Latin America and in the United States. If no proposals were made of any kind, if there was no prospect of any talks, then I came to the conclusion that the situation would inevitably deteriorate. The proposal, which we floated, and which even now seems to me a perfectly credible negotiating tactic, was to suggest that, rather on the lines of Hong Kong, we should accept the Argentinean claim to sovereignty but negotiate a very long lease of 100 years or more, which would guarantee the continuance of the Falkland Islanders' livelihood, nationality and integrity. The world a hundred or two hundred years ahead would be a very different place. I have no idea whether this would have worked out or not, or whether it would have been acceptable to the Argentine, but it would certainly have been an issue on which we could negotiate and prolong those negotiations to a point which would at least postpone any drastic action on the part of the Argentineans.

Such a tactic was completely unacceptable to large numbers in the House of Commons. Those on the right maintained that it was intolerable to suggest that a British colony should be handed over to a foreign country, quite regardless of any possible lease. Those on the left vociferously objected to a proposal which handed over any British territory to a fascist dictator. The lease proposal died amidst a great deal of acrimony and with it died the prospect of any serious negotiation with Argentina. We all know the consequences of this. No government could have survived the understandable feeling of humiliation of the electorate if there had not been a resolute attempt to recapture the islands. This in no way detracts from the courage and determination shown by Margaret Thatcher, particularly since I remember from my days at the Ministry of Defence that successive Chiefs of Staff had given an opinion that the recapture of the islands, if an Argentinean invasion has been successful, would have been extremely difficult, if not impossible. Incidentally, the success of the Falklands conflict enabled Margaret Thatcher to win the next election by an overwhelming majority. Before the Falklands it would have been extremely doubtful that she and her government could have survived.

What then are the lessons, if any, to be learnt from that episode? In my judgement, the cause of this conflict was the split in both parties as to whether or not there should be a continuation of negotiations and the basis on which they should be conducted and, of course, the lack of understanding of the consequences of an end to negotiations. The reception of the lease-back proposal was so hostile and the support of the moderates so lukewarm that at any rate, at the time, it seemed pointless to pursue the proposals. Perhaps in hindsight we should have tried harder, though I do not think it would have made any difference, and it must be said that the Cabinet itself was fairly half hearted. I also think, in hindsight, that we, or possibly I, relied too much on intelligence reports about what the likely intentions were as opposed to ascertainable facts such as military capabilities and dispositions.

Intelligence passed to me was that there would be no recourse to armed intervention until all avenues of mediation had been tried and in particular until procedures in the United Nations had been exhausted. It is, of course, very difficult, and I note this in light of some fairly recent events, to make a judgement about the intentions of a potential adversary as opposed to hard facts. It must be a matter of judgement and is very difficult indeed. But when you are dealing with a dictator and a dictator who was in considerable domestic difficulty, it is unwise to assume that a military adventure, which would probably be popular and divert attention from his problems at home, would not be an attractive option for a desperate man to adopt.

One more lesson to be learnt from the three-year period when I was Foreign Secretary was in relation to Europe. We, the British, were in dispute with the rest of the European Community about the British budgetary contribution, which again must sound very familiar. Though the previous government had valiantly tried to resolve the problem, there had been no result, except increasing acrimony between ourselves and our European friends. I remember very well how much I wanted to improve our relations with Europe, but the budgetary problem bedevilled our relations then and perhaps even now.

In my judgement, our European friends were much too inflexible in their attitude to our problem, for there was no doubt that we had right on our side and we were paying far too much in comparison with others at that time, whose economies were much stronger than ours. After all, if we had decided that we were not prepared to pay, they would anyway have had to pick up the bill. The Prime Minister, Mrs Thatcher, was absolutely determined that we would not be browbeaten into accepting the status quo or an inadequate compromise and this she made very clear. Indeed, you may remember an occasion, widely publicised during a European Summit, in which she declared in no uncertain terms: 'I want my money back!' This attitude was considered by a number of those who were not always in agreement with the Prime Minister's policy to be a rather strident demand made to such an august diplomatic international assembly; certainly the leaders of France and Germany were inclined, then and afterwards, to raise their eyebrows at her determination not to be railroaded to an acceptance of something which was not, in her judgement, in the country's interest and the rather positive way in which she made that plain. All I can say is that had she not been as resolute and as single minded as she was, we would not have come to the satisfactory conclusion that was eventually reached. Of course, there was blood on the floor afterwards, but it was a very good example in international affairs of someone taking a position which they believed to be right, and being prepared to press their case until they were successful. The grudging respect for her at that time, together with her fortitude over the Falklands, stood us in good stead as a country during the years of her Prime Ministership.

Lastly, I would like to focus on the question of the break-up of Yugoslavia and the subsequent events. I will explain what the position was at that time and why I became involved. I do not think that the break-up of Yugoslavia would have occurred if the confrontation between East and West still existed, but it did not. Tito died and Marxism died too. The chief ministers of several republics, detaching themselves from the centre and, incidentally, from a constitution which the redoubtable Tito had devised and was unworkable, had become nationalists in their own republics rather than communists. This development took place immediately in the aftermath of the Gulf

War. The Americans took the view that, having resolved that question, and taken the overwhelming lead in doing so, the Yugoslav problem, which was a European problem, should be the responsibility of the European Union.

The European Union took the view that it would be greatly to the advantage of the stability of Europe if Yugoslavia remained one country; the break-up might lead to difficulties on the fringes of Europe, in particular the erstwhile Soviet republics. Consequently they suggested that there should be a constitutional conference and asked me to take the chair. Historically, before the formation of Yugoslavia, the Europeans had been divided in their attitude to the Serbs and Croats. The Germans and Austrians, for historical reasons, were always supportive of the Croats. Indeed, the Germans during the Second World War gave Croatia independence for the first time in its history. The French, on the other hand, had always been supporters of the Serbs. Consequently, there was no consensus in the European Community as to who was right or who was wrong. It is interesting to speculate how the EU's Foreign Minister, if such a post is ever established, would have coped – or indeed with recent European divisions on Iraq. Thus the Europeans were divided. The Serbs should be condemned for invading Croatia – equally the Croatians should be condemned for declaring their independence without any safeguards for the 600,000 Serbs who lived in their country. Memories are long and the Serbs remember the execution and exile of so many of the 1.2 million Serbs who were living in Croatia in 1942. It seemed to me that the only way in which the entity of Yugoslavia could be preserved was as a federal state, in which the republics could decide how far they wanted to integrate with the federal authority: some more, some less.

Although the war was raging between Serbia and Croatia, the conference got under way and we made some progress, though the sticking point was clearly going to be the attitude of Slobodan Milošević, who, whatever his failings may have been, was prepared to say 'yes' or 'no' and stick to it, unlike his Croatian counterpart,

President Franjo Tudman, who almost invariably did the opposite of what he had promised.

I do not know whether, if the conference had continued, we would have been successful; very probably not, given the character of those involved, but there was no opportunity to find out. The Germans decided they wished to recognise as independent countries Croatia and Slovenia; this proposal was accepted by the European Foreign Ministers, after a discussion in which those opposed to this barely raised their voices. This spelt the end of the conference. If Croatia was independent, the Serbs and others were no longer interested in any federal proposals or any constitutional conference. More importantly, if the European Union was prepared to recognise the independence of Croatia, it had to offer independence to the other republics and in particular, Bosnia. The Bosnians had had a referendum in which the Bosnian Serbs had made it plain that they were not prepared to accept an independent Bosnia under the constitution as it stood. And in that constitution they, and the other parties, had a right of veto. Consequently, an offer of independence to Bosnia, which President Izetbegović could hardly refuse, must inevitably lead to a civil war – and so it did, as, incidentally, I told the European Union ministers it would. What followed will be known to all who read this: NATO intervention, United Nations intervention, American intervention and, in the end, the Dayton Agreement, which was almost identical to a proposal that José Cutileiro and I made three years previously. But then, at that time, as I pointed out in what I mentioned above about Zimbabwe, all parties, for one reason or another, wanted a settlement.

What lessons, then, can we draw from this dismal episode? I suppose if you stand back and look at it objectively, the intervention by the Europeans, far from resolving the problems, made them much worse. If there had been no European involvement, there would have been much less ethnic cleansing and far fewer casualties; it would all have been over in a comparatively short space of time, since both Milošević and Tudman told me separately that they had agreed between them to carve

Bosnia up; the Bosnian Muslims would have been the sacrifice for that quick solution. But I do not think it would have been possible for the European Union not to become involved. To ignore a war on our doorsteps and the consequences that might flow from it was not a credible option. But peacekeeping and peacemaking in this particular situation proved very difficult. The effort to be neutral and not take sides left the three warring participants convinced that we favoured the others. Much the same was true of the United Nations peacekeeping force. An added obstacle was the decision to send a United Nations force to keep the peace that was expressly forbidden to use their arms, except in self-defence. A grave mistake, compounded by the declaration of 'safe areas'. These were not safe.

The broader lessons from this episode are that if intervention in a civil war or a Yugoslavia situation is necessary, it is very much better that we should know whose side we are on and act accordingly. Umpires in white coats in that sort of situation are in an impossible position. As Lord Slim recalls, during a riot at the Red Fort in Delhi, a young soldier turned to his sergeant and said: 'What did he mean by neutral, Sergeant?' 'Neutral, my lad,' replied the sergeant, 'means that when you go down that adjectival bazaar you're just as likely to be hit by a Mohammedan brick as by a Hindu brick.'

Secondly, to send soldiers to keep the peace with the sort of instruction they were given in Yugoslavia is unfair on them and can lead to real trouble. Furthermore, to send a United Nations force or a NATO force in to keep the peace, with the strict instructions that they could only use their weapons to defend themselves, whilst at the same time announcing that there are safe areas guarded by these forces, was not only misleading to those who thought the area was safe, but led to some of the nastiest instances in the whole of the war.

One last reflection. I am quite a lot older then my colleagues who have contributed to this series. Almost an endangered species! Apart from the last twelve years or so, as a boy, a young man and an adult, I have lived all my life in the shadows of a world war. I was at Sandhurst at the time of Munich and in the army before the war. I remember well how ill equipped we were and my astonishment that the threat of war did not apparently spur the government of the day into doing something about it. After six years of war and success, we realised that we faced just as dangerous and threatening an enemy. The Cold War lasted over fifty years. We lived with the threat of a disastrous nuclear war which, on occasion, seemed very close. There was, however, one positive feature. The potential horrors of a nuclear war imposed a discipline upon all of us, not just East and West but on the Third World as well. The rivalry between the two power blocs spilt over into the underdeveloped countries and both superpowers sought to influence the non-aligned countries.

The rivalry between the superpowers imposed a discipline on all of us, in case a spark in one part of the world would set off a nuclear explosion, which would engulf the whole world. Just to give one example, if the Cold War had continued, there would have been no break-up of Yugoslavia. Their leaders would have calculated that the Soviet Union might decide to move in to secure ports on the Adriatic, a situation which the Americans would certainly not have accepted and with catastrophic consequences. The break-up of the Soviet Union changed everything. There was now only one superpower with the military, industrial and economic power to influence and indeed to control events. However unwillingly, the United Sates took on the role of the world's policeman. They did so in Kuwait and masterminded a political and military coalition to help them. Initially, they left the problem of Yugoslavia to the Europeans. It was, I believe, only the American intervention that in the end enabled a solution to be found. We should be immensely grateful to them.

Recent events in Iraq have proved much more difficult, both for the Americans and Europeans. In the event, the Americans, with a few allies, went ahead, despite the vigorous protests of some of their closest European allies. I do not want to discuss the rights or wrongs of what the Americans or French or Germans did. I understand the irritation of our American allies at what was said and done in Europe. I understand too the nervousness of those who opposed the war as American unilateralism. What has been done is done. What is important now is to repair the damage. As one who believes passionately in the importance of Atlantic relations and the global stability that such a relationship brings, this is all-important. No country, however powerful, can indefinitely go it alone. Friends and allies are necessary. As for the Europeans, they must understand the problems which face the world policeman. When we ran the world in the nineteenth century, we were cordially disliked. No one likes a dominant power. Jealousy and hostility, not gratitude, was our experience. There must be understanding on both sides. The sooner the rift is healed, the sooner the world will be a safer place.

The Rt Hon. the Lord Howe of Aberavon CH QC

Foreign Secretary June 1983–July 1989

'Politics and personality in the Thatcher years'

Based on a lecture given at the London School of Economics
and Political Science, 21 October 2003

More perhaps than any other job in government, being Foreign Secretary is perceived to concern the management of what the Chinese call 'problems left over by history'. The phrase in fact conveys some very misleading impressions of the real agenda. First, because 'problems' is probably the wrong word, simply because that word implies the existence of a solution. And second, because the phrase 'left over by history' again suggests an ordered array of problems waiting to be picked up and dealt with consecutively. Real life, of course, is much less orderly than that. Only a minority of diplomatic problems actually achieve, or can hope to achieve, a solution. Many of them have to be managed, some almost indefinitely, in the context of some other quite different, broader relationship. Often one can do little more than set the problem on course to what one day might be a solution. And some problems, of course, burst from a clear blue sky on a wholly innocent Foreign Secretary, like the fatwa on Salman Rushdie, which emerged on St Valentine's Day 1989. I heard about it at dawn, so to speak, and by lunchtime I had to have completed reading *The Satanic Verses* so that I could talk about it on *The World at One*. It is that kind of thing which takes you by surprise.

One very striking feature about all these things is the extent to which what happens depends crucially upon the composition of the group of ministers, diplomats, other professionals, who have to decide on their reaction. Sometimes the input of a particular diplomat or professional can be absolutely critical. More often it's the experience, the temperament, the mood of the politicians that is more decisive. Finally, the politics of an event plays a determining role. Only when all elements – politics, professionalism and the personalities involved – work in harmony is there a chance to come to a positive outcome.

In light of that analysis, I think I was quite fortunate, at least in some respects, in the timing of my own arrival at the Foreign and Commonwealth Office because by that time, June 1983, I had been working in partnership with the Prime Minister, Margaret Thatcher, for eight full years, covering my time as shadow Chancellor and Chancellor. We were almost halfway through our time together, halfway towards the conclusion of our quasi-matrimonial relationship. By the time I joined her at the Foreign Office, the Prime Minister had been engaged in top level foreign policy decision-making for four years. She had demonstrated star quality of a remarkable kind. I am sure some people reading this may have been with us when we went to the Tokyo economic summit in summer 1979. In those days all heads of government had to give separate statements to the press conference. It was a feast of competitive rhetoric and in Tokyo, because of the astonishment of Japanese womanhood at the existence of a female Prime Minister, the hall was packed with wives, secretaries and other hangers-on of diplomats, journalists and all the rest, gazing open eyed at this phenomenon. Margaret Thatcher, because she was the new kid on the block, made the last of the prepared statements. She had to be followed by the hapless Roy Jenkins as President of the European Commission and she was the only one who did not speak from a script. She spoke extemporarily (although she had thought very carefully about it) and it was an absolute wow. People realised then that we had got a totally new phenomenon in this leader and I think that it's very important to understand that. Moreover, she had been guided, by the time I joined her, through her first four years by Peter Carrington, a Foreign Secretary with enormous experience.

By that same date even I had ceased to be a complete novice in the wider world, because I had been minister of trade in the Heath government and, as Chancellor of the Exchequer, I had attended a number of summits. Moreover, I had attended many high level meetings in Europe, presided over two or three realignments of the European Monetary System and had become chairman of the IMF Interim Committee. All of that had given me some feel for international affairs.

By the time the Prime Minister and this Foreign Secretary got into joint harness in 1983, we were both reasonably mature creatures, both quite worldly wise and still – in those early post-Treasury days – quite harmonious. We were a well-adjusted partnership, seven years still to go before the break-up of our relationship. Much that we did achieve, or worked at anyway, was governed by the balance of that relationship. After giving this chapter its title, I realised that probably a better title could have been borrowed from Nigel Nicolson, if I had decided to call it 'Portrait of a Marriage'.

We started off, inevitably, focused upon the Cold War. History could scarcely have bequeathed a greater problem. Not least because at that time, Margaret Thatcher was cast as the Iron Lady, shoulder to shoulder with Ronald Reagan and confronting the 'evil empire'. People expected a generation of further confrontation. Happily, we had a brief interval before this problem came to a head. At that time George Shultz, the American Secretary of State, had been in office for about twelve months. In June 1983 we were to find ourselves both singing the same kind of mood music. George Shultz told the Congress that 'our fundamental and common interest in the avoidance of war impels us to work towards a relationship that can lead to a safer world for all mankind'.[1] That was a mature judgement of enormous importance, which I shared. It was exactly to that end that in the first week of July I convened a meeting of officials and ministers to try and see exactly where we went along that road. We all felt that the United States might finally be moving away from a mode in which she had no apparent interest in the Soviet Union, except to defame her. In those circumstances, some of us dared to think that Britain could hardly be better placed to take advantage of any opportunities that might open up. It should be possible for Britain to play a significant part perhaps in weakening the Soviet grip on eastern Europe, even perhaps encouraging some positive changes in the Soviet Union itself.

So we concluded our seminar of Foreign Office and other officials with an action programme of some twenty points. We didn't know how that would play at No. 10 but, very remarkably, almost at the same time, we got the message that the Prime Minister would herself welcome a broader, two-day seminar at Chequers attended by academics with expertise in the Soviet Union, as well as the rest of us, to study that topic in particular, along with other foreign policy topics.

We arranged a meeting at Chequers for 8 and 9 September 1983. The timing was actually extremely well chosen because just one week before we met, the Korean Air Lines airliner 007 with 269 passengers on board was shot down without warning in the Sea of Japan by Soviet fighter aircraft. Equally by chance, four days after that I was to have my first meeting at a CSCE meeting in Madrid with that great figure Andrei Gromyko, the Soviet Foreign Minister. I have to say the meeting fell well short of being a success. It was brusque, bad tempered and entirely fruitless. When I got to the seminar at Chequers, it was very tempting to argue that dialogue with this creature and the regime he represented was entirely useless and pointless. Happily, we took the opposite view. It seemed to me that Gromyko's brutally unpromising performance powerfully reinforced my instinct, that we needed desperately to look for fresh ways of getting through to the Soviet leadership. Gradually in our discussion, that view became crystallised between all of us at the Chequers meeting.

It was agreed that once the Korean Air Lines crisis had died down, we should seek ways of improving the links of communication with the Soviet leadership. Margaret Thatcher characteristically attached conditions to that. They illustrated the balance of the discussion. This search should go on so long, she said, as she was not herself involved in it. And secondly, she would retain the right to intervene to veto the process if it seemed that talks were 'going too far'. So there was a fairly cautious signal to go ahead. But it did give us the essential go-ahead we wanted and we realised of course, that it was going to take time.

So the politics of where we intended to go were clear. We did touch on a number of other problems, mainly those left over by imperial history; I won't go into those here because each of them might take some time, ranging from the Falklands to Cyprus and Gibraltar. Rather I will focus on developments between the United Kingdom and the United States.

We lost no time, in fact, in presenting our fresh approach to the United States. Just two or three weeks later, Margaret Thatcher was addressing the Winston Churchill Foundation in Washington and gave them the clear message: 'We live on the same planet; we must be ready, therefore, and we are, if and when the Soviet leadership is ready, to commence talks with the Soviet leadership.'[2] Less than two weeks later, we were both together on the platform of the Conservative Party conference. As it happened, I was presiding over the proceedings when Margaret Thatcher delivered her wide-ranging closing speech. In the course of this, she was talking about our attitude towards the Soviet Union and I saw how she broke away from her well-marked script at one important point. When she talked about arms control, she looked at the audience without the script and said, 'As I am sure you will understand, there is no one more anxious for genuine disarmament than the person who bears the ultimate responsibility for the nuclear deterrent in our own country.'[3] It was a very moving moment to find her ad-libbing to that personal extent and committing her sincerity to the pursuit of a way forward on that important subject.

And we did indeed set about presenting the case. She did in fact have her first visit behind the Iron Curtain, to Hungary, within six months, and that whetted her appetite for more.

My own first visit to Moscow, the first visit by a Foreign Secretary for seven years, apart from going to funerals, took place in July 1984. Once again I had six hours with Gromyko. I did try to raise with him, as on other occasions, the question of human rights. On that occasion his response was quite simple: 'You're lowering the tone of our conversation.' It remained like that and set the tone of the entire encounter. But off stage, alongside our political endeavours, our professionals were also hard at work trying to see where we went next. We had been trying to identify the man most likely to succeed the hapless Konstantin

Chernenko, the fragile, short-lived successor to Andropov.[4] The Soviet Department at the Foreign Office, in concert with the intelligence services, were picking up, for example, messages from our Tokyo post about conversations there between Prime Minister Trudeau[5] and Mr Georgi Arbatov of the Soviet Union. We were getting similarly useful tips from Mr Oleg Gordievsky (second in command of the KGB post in the London embassy, who was happily working on our side).

As a consequence of this kind of meticulous analysis, I had been able, when I went to Moscow to see Gromyko, to take with me an even more important document than the brief on how to handle him. For I had taken with me an invitation from the chairman of our House of Commons Foreign Affairs Committee, Sir Anthony Kershaw, to his opposite number in the Soviet Union, the chairman of the Soviet Foreign Affairs Committee and youngest member of the Politburo, 52-year-old Mikhail Gorbachev. This was the man whom we had (correctly) identified as the one most worthwhile influencing so far as the future was concerned. And the acceptance of that invitation was due, I think, to two factors. One, because it contained a well-directed political message from Margaret Thatcher, who was already recognised as an important player in this scene, and two, because it was based upon a well-crafted diplomatic analysis. Our team had designed an invitation which would be very hard to refuse. So the politics were right and the professionalism was right. The third component had yet to become evident. That was the interpersonal chemistry between the two personalities involved.

Mikhail Gorbachev arrived at Chequers on 16 December 1984 for lunch and afternoon discussions. I spent four hours with Mikhail Gorbachev and Margaret Thatcher and the interpreters. It was an extraordinary experience, because the communication between the two of them was so effective and so direct and so instant, that the interpreters became, as they can sometimes do, virtually invisible. One was engaged witnessing real communication between people. Mikhail Gorbachev had a spontaneity and engaging style, quoting from his own notes in his own rather diffident manuscript book, quoting Palmerston to us. Immediately one realised one was dealing with a Soviet citizen of a kind we had never seen before. Margaret Thatcher, unsurprisingly, was fluent, but measured, thoughtful and manifestly sincere. Again she came to the same central message: if Palmerston made the point that Britain has no permanent friends and no permanent enemies, but only permanent interests, then it echoed her message that we live on the same planet and we must find ways of living together on that same planet. And that was the message that Gorbachev had brought with him as well. The interpersonal chemistry of their relationship was crucial to the outcome, and by the end of that afternoon, Margaret Thatcher made the classic statement, he is 'a man with whom I can do business'. Note the 'I'! There were in fact only two or perhaps three people to whom Margaret had an immensely deferential attitude. One of them, perhaps surprisingly, was King Hussein, the most courteous man I have ever encountered. Margaret, in the presence of King Hussein, was bowing to him, and 'Your Majesty' this and 'Your Excellency' that. That was one, but the other two she deferred to were Ronald Reagan and Mikhail Gorbachev. I think that set of personal relationships, her success in commending the two of them to each other, was probably the most important achievement in the whole field of foreign affairs in her life.

Not, of course, that that was the only factor. People, I think, tend to overlook the importance of Eduard Shevardnadze. Eduard Shevardnadze emerged from nowhere as far as we were concerned, to replace Andrei Gromyko for the Helsinki Final Act tenth anniversary in July 1985. He first appeared at Helsinki. Early on I was able to learn a bit more about him, in a strange way, from the Mozambican Foreign Minister, Joaquim Chissano, when he met me at the airport in Maputo and we talked, as one does on those often rather stilted occasions, about our experiences. He had just come back from Moscow and he described his time in Moscow with Shevardnadze. At the end of their talks Shevardnadze said, 'Well, we're due to go to the Bolshoi for the evening now, but maybe you don't want to, because I'd quite like to talk to you.'

And Chissano said, 'I'd like that too.' So they spent the entire evening together, with Shevardnadze asking questions which Gromyko would never have asked, questioning Chissano about what he thought was wrong about the Soviet Union's policies towards Africa. And this was, again, an insight that was quite remarkable. Very shortly after that Shevardnadze was making equally remarkable speeches to his own diplomatic people. I'll quote just one sentence from one of them: 'The image of a state is in its attitude towards its own citizens, recognition of the sovereignty of the individual.'[6] And that wasn't just being made for public consumption; it was made to his own diplomatic professionals.

The other fact that one must never overlook was the collective solidarity and wisdom of NATO and the European Union at that time. Shultz made a remarkable leader of the sixteen Foreign Ministers of NATO. But there were other people, like the West German Foreign Minister, Hans-Dietrich Genscher, for example, who had a lot of experience. All this made a great contribution to the strength which we brought together to the management of the Soviet Union.

Turning to a less grand stage will demonstrate that the same ingredients mattered, the three ingredients I've talked about: getting the politics right, having the professionalism supporting those politics right and having the right personality mix. This was the case, to our good fortune, in the Anglo-Irish relationship. There was also a bit of luck about that, because we happened to have recently become members of the European Community together. Until then British and Irish ministers didn't even say hello to each other. But once we had joined the European Community, we began sitting alongside each other discussing common interests there. In December 1980, four ministers from the UK government, Prime Minister Thatcher, Foreign Secretary Carrington, myself as Chancellor and Humphrey Atkins, the Northern Ireland Secretary, went to Dublin to attend an unprecedented Anglo-Irish summit, which was held at Dublin Castle. We realised that this was the first time British Cabinet ministers had been in the Irish Free State or the Irish Republic since it had been established. I remember one episode quite clearly from that occasion. I was put to sit next to an Irish Treasury official, and during the course of lunch he turned to me and said, 'How do you like the claret, then, Sir Geoffrey?' I said, 'I like it very much indeed. It's very good.' 'So you should,' he said, 'at £84 a bottle.' I realised then that treasury officials were the same the world over, where price was the only thing that mattered.

But it was that chance coming together, and the fact that the Irish electorate were in a rather oscillatory mood at that time, putting Garret FitzGerald into office, taking him out again, and back in again several times, that gave him just enough opportunities to make bright suggestions to Margaret Thatcher as to what should happen next. He met her in 1981 and suggested the establishment of an Anglo-Irish intergovernmental council. Never heard of before, it was a crucial component to everything that happened next. The council consisted of the two governments' Cabinet Secretaries – on our own side, Robert Armstrong, one of the most experienced and well-judged Cabinet Secretaries that I can remember, and with him a deputy secretary from the Foreign Office who was in the Cabinet Office, David Goodall, who was himself a very industrious member of an old Anglo-Irish family and very reflective. We thus had in place this group of senior officials on both sides, for all the years that lay ahead. We took the whole process forward with comparable opposite numbers and a very committed, very professional, diplomatic structure, in continuous existence through rough and smooth.

Above all, we had this extraordinary combination of personalities. Garret FitzGerald was one of the most irrepressible, enthusiastic and engaging people with whom I've had to deal. He met Margaret Thatcher again, when he was back in office, at the European Summit in Stuttgart in the summer of 1983. 'Margaret,' he said, 'isn't it time we began having some substantive talks about all this?' He describes Margaret's reaction as being immediately receptive. Both Prime Ministers became intensely engaged in this relationship, for quite different reasons. FitzGerald's concern was to get something done, to engage the minority community, who were completely alienated from the government structure, in the affairs of Northern Ireland. Every time he said to Margaret, 'They're alienated,' she said, 'Stop using that awful word, Garret. It's a Marxist word and I don't like to hear you using it.' But it was his case and he was going to make it.

Margaret's interest was quite different. She was determined not to betray the Unionist community and above all to enhance their security. There was thus a fascinating, episodic relationship with Garret FitzGerald, who was always the driving force, carrying the process forward. At the same time Margaret Thatcher deserves real credit for her readiness to rise to the historic challenge. The politics of all this were under constant discussion at Cabinet level (in a way that I think hardly takes place today). Within our government these issues were being considered not just by the generality of Cabinet but by people like William Whitelaw, who had had experience as Northern Ireland Secretary, and Quintin Hailsham, whose family had had a long connection with Ulster. The continuity of officials marched alongside a continuing interest on the part of the politicians. I like to think that a little added continuity was achieved due to the existence of a certain Welsh Foreign Secretary. During my time at the Foreign Office there were no less than three different Northern Ireland Secretaries: Jim Prior first of all, then Douglas Hurd and Tom King. Each new one who arrived understandably received a reinjection, through the Northern Ireland Office in Belfast, of Unionist scepticism of the process. Alongside all three of them there was at least the continuo of a Welshman, who had some insight into the importance of other people's patriotism.

One of the things that Margaret didn't find easy to understand was the concept that other people like herself could be patriotic in their own way. I think that I've always been able to do that as a Welshman. When I go to my native land in Wales, if I am there for any length of time, I get fed up with the parochialism of some of the people I am dealing with. But as soon as I get off the train at Paddington and am back in

London I begin to rail at the patronising attitudes of the English. I felt I could convey something of that to Margaret, as to the way in which the Irish thought about us.

We did arrive at the Anglo-Irish Agreement in 1985. That was another example of the triumph of her head over her heart. The fact is that Margaret was prepared to be persuaded to achieve an agreement, albeit with some reluctance. In some of her later writings she has actually said that the outcome had been disappointing. 'It is surely time', she said, 'to consider an alternative approach.'[7] However, it was her commitment and her personality which carried the day with the Unionist community.

I come now to another component of this historic legacy, another of the obstacles constructed for Foreign Secretaries by their predecessors, namely Hong Kong. This was a problem whose priority had long been foreseen – a 99-year lease expiring on 30 June 1997 – and one where we had a singularly weak hand. We claimed title to the freehold of 8 per cent of Hong Kong, as a result of a treaty we imposed upon the Chinese in the mid-nineteenth century. We claimed no more than a leasehold to 92 per cent of it on the basis of a second, similar treaty, which the Chinese government in Beijing challenged as unequal and invalid. We had one valid and important card, namely the prosperous condition of Hong Kong. If China wished to recover Hong Kong, she wished also to recover it in working order, and was understandably reluctant to risk destroying it. It was a set of negotiations where once again the head had to overrule the heart, if we were to get the right outcome.

We were able to get the right diplomatic resources in place. The long sequence of British officials as governors of Hong Kong, from Murray MacLehose to Edward Youde and David Wilson, and ambassadors to China, perhaps most notably of all Percy Cradock, were people who had a real insight into China. The Hong Kong Department in the Foreign Office expanded during the two years of our negotiations from a strength of three to twenty-three people. During this period they received 4,000 telegrams from Beijing and Hong Kong about the progress of negotiations, and despatched 2,400 telegrams back. The professionalism was firmly in place.

Equally the politics was in place too. We all had no doubt – Margaret Thatcher and the rest of our colleagues – on the need to find an outcome for the future of Hong Kong that would preserve that which was good about it. We had a very effective constant triangle of consultation. We were working in a Cabinet committee which met quite regularly in Downing Street. At the same time we were in close consultation with the Executive Council in Hong Kong, through our governor. The Hong Kong ExCo came to London several times a year, and I was going to Hong Kong with the same kind of frequency. We were holding debates in Parliament in Westminster and regular press conferences in Hong Kong.

The personalities here were quite different because, perhaps more than in any other relationship, Britain had contrived to produce what worked as a hard cop, soft cop relationship. Margaret Thatcher had met Deng Xiaoping only once, in Beijing in September 1982, just a few months after the St Paul's service of thanksgiving for the reacquisition of the Falkland Islands. Hence the topic that was at the top of her mind was sovereignty and our entitlement to the sovereignty of Hong Kong. A robust exchange took place between Margaret Thatcher and Deng Xiaoping, which resulted in some rather unhelpful conclusions. Deng Xiaoping set a two-year limit for the close of negotiations. 'This must be finished by September 1984,' he said. Margaret Thatcher, in an interview in the plane on the way back to Hong Kong from Beijing, said that she cast grave doubt on the Chinese willingness to respect any treaty – those that existed and any one they might sign in the future. Relations were not exactly warm at that time. It left the Chinese in no doubt that I, as Foreign Secretary, was having to handle a rather 'difficult' client.

By contrast, but only by contrast, they must have found me a fairly approachable advocate. As the end of the two years approached, we were trying to grapple for the key components of the elaborate document, which we finally agreed upon. We were converting Deng Xiaoping's four words 'one country, two systems', which he later elaborated into about ten sentences, into a fourteen-, fifteen-, sixteen-page document. This document became the Joint Declaration for the Future of Hong Kong. We had to fight for every inch of it. Rather remarkably the Chinese deadline was working interestingly in our favour. For in the last few days of those negotiations, we slipped in two very important bids for what we wanted in the concluding document. And they were both conceded. The Legislative Council 'shall be constituted by elections', and the Executive 'shall be accountable to the legislature'. A few days before the deadline we were able to get both of those into the agreement, quite possibly because the Chinese negotiators felt that we were being pressed by my difficulty in getting the case sold to my 'client', the Prime Minister!

For a long time, as can be seen, the three Ps – politics, professionalism, personalities – remained in comfortable relationship with each other. In the end, however, two topics working almost in tandem illustrated the decline in my working relationship with the Prime Minister. The first was transatlantic relations, and the second, of course, was Europe.

Relations with the United States certainly did change in their nature during my time working together with Margaret Thatcher. They were tested by various episodes. First of all, quite early on in my time at the Foreign Office in October 1983, the United States decided to send troops into the tiny state of Grenada without any effective consultation with us. They had decided to do so at a meeting in Atlanta, Georgia on Saturday morning, 22 October 1983. They assured us throughout the weekend, in response to our enquiries in Washington, that they had no such plans. We had a meeting of ministers at 10.30 on the Monday morning, and agreed with their conclusion – in the form in which it had been disclosed to us. It wouldn't make sense, we thought, for any troops to be sent into the island. I informed the House of Commons at 3.30

that afternoon accordingly. At seven o'clock that evening we got a telegram from the White House saying that the Americans were planning to send their troops in and asking us whether we could offer them our advice. Margaret Thatcher and I met and asked officials to prepare a cautious reply. As it happened, the Prime Minister and I then went out to separate dinners. I went to dine with the American Bankers' Association, in the presence of the American minister in the embassy. Margaret went to dine with somebody in the Royal Household, in the presence of the American ambassador, neither of whom knew anything about what was afoot.

By the time we got back to 10 Downing Street at eleven o'clock, a second telegram had arrived, saying that the troops were indeed going in at first light the following morning. Margaret Thatcher thereupon telephoned Ronald Reagan and, so we're told, he had to hold the telephone some distance from his ear. But the die had been cast – and the interesting thing, as I gathered later from George Shultz himself, is that it was a quite deliberate decision not to inform us, because of his fear that if Margaret Thatcher had got at Ronald Reagan before the decision had been taken, she would have dissuaded him from doing it. It was a very disturbing experience and our reaction – Margaret Thatcher's and my own – at that time was one of great dismay and indeed real anger. We had to try to present the relationship with the United States in its usual comfortable fashion whilst at the same time displaying our anger at what had happened. David Steel commented that the Foreign Secretary had managed to achieve a unique feat by coming down on both sides of the fence at the same time. One other chap who took the same view later on was the Singapore Prime Minister, Lee Kuan Yew. When we discussed the Grenada episode at the Delhi Commonwealth conference a few weeks later, you may imagine there were very different opinions. Mr Julius Nyerere[8] had much to say in favour of the American attitude, because it was in line with what he had done with his intervention in Uganda. He had removed Obote from that country. Mr Mugabe, on the other hand, had no sympathy with it, because it was in line with what he feared the South Africans might do to him. Lee Kuan Yew was able, as always, to crown the proceedings, by saying that the Americans shouldn't have done it but he was very glad they did. That was the first episode in which Margaret Thatcher's reaction and mine were very much along the same lines.

On 5 April 1986 the West Berlin nightclub La Belle, a favourite with American servicemen, was bombed by Libyan special agents, killing two American servicemen. When the Americans proposed to retaliate for the bombing of the nightclub in Berlin by bombing Libya, we had to react at quite short notice. Margaret's and my reactions throughout that were along the same lines. We were still working closely together. The Americans, as sometimes happens, said, 'We've got to have a response to this.' The word 'response' features quite often in American political vocabulary as a euphemism for 'retaliation'. Certainly, that doesn't have a very strong place in diplomatic affairs. So we worked for a long time, three or four days, to persuade them that we did believe there was a legitimate case for action against the Libyan regime, because we had no doubt about their responsibility for the bombing. But that case had to be founded on self-defence. Only on that basis could we justify the use of American air bases in the UK for the bombing of Gaddafi and his headquarters in order to deter Gaddafi from doing the same thing in the future. Eventually we got the Americans to formulate the case in that way, to limit the nature of the attack they were going to embark on and to avoid too much collateral damage. Even so, I was much criticised in the House of Commons and by most of the press for what I had said and for what we had done. It couldn't be justified, they said. As the months passed, people began to say, well, it seems to have worked. It becomes more and more difficult to criticise actions taken in self-defence when they have been successful in defending you.

One of my predecessors was an innocent victim, if you like, of that process. During the debates in the House of Commons one of those who criticised our conduct most vigorously at the time was none other than David Owen. When both of us took part in a television broadcast three days after 9/11, we were discussing whether the United States was entitled to take any action in response to 9/11. Before I had begun to speak, David Owen began saying, 'Well, of course, they're entitled to take action in self-defence, as you remember they were at the time of Libya.' And I said, 'But hang on, that's not what you said in 1986.' Later on that day, in a debate in the House of Lords, Owen acknowledged that his position previously had been opposed to the US action.[9] This episode was another example of our minds – Margaret's and mine – working together.

I think we began to move apart, strangely, in relation to the Strategic Defence Initiative (SDI), also known as Star Wars, which became a very hot issue in the early part of 1985. The division between Prime Minister and Foreign Secretary was probably due, as much as anything else, to the fact that I am, and had been for twenty years of my life, a practising lawyer. Whereas Margaret Thatcher was, although a qualified lawyer, also a scientist. I think her scientific reaction was attracted by the subtlety, the complexity, the potential of the SDI, while I was much more cautious. I was candid, perhaps unwise, enough in a speech I made at that time, to question the concept as being like 'the creation of a Maginot line in space', a phrase that stirred Richard Perle[10] to intense wrath against me, and didn't altogether endear me to the American administration.[11] A month earlier, on 20 February, Margaret Thatcher had addressed both houses of Congress. In her memoirs she wrote, 'I used my speech to give strong support for SDI. I had a terrific reception.'[12] And she did indeed. I was there to witness the standing ovation which she received from Congress. I have to say, and this is perhaps also relevant today, that nothing is more calculated to impair the judgement of a British Prime Minister than a standing ovation from both houses of Congress.

Europe again offers a rather similar sequence of stories. It's easy to forget that for a number of years, the Thatcher–Howe partnership successfully managed some quite difficult questions. We were able to solve the 'bloody British budget question', as Roy Jenkins called it, at Fontainebleau on a very satisfactory basis. Margaret displayed her characteristic self-confidence at this EU summit. We were finally offered a deal by President Mitterrand that would entitle the UK to a refund of two-thirds of our contribution. We had been campaigning from the outset for a 66 per cent rebate. As a fairly experienced trial lawyer, I was prepared to think that 65 per cent and 66 per cent were pretty well interchangeable. Margaret Thatcher said no, we must get our 66 per cent. We went back to the Council Chamber and the debate took place. We got our 66 per cent, which was worth £150 million over the next ten years. So who was right?

We also succeeded in negotiating the Single European Act in 1985–6, which effectively laid the foundations for the completion of the single market. It involved an extension of qualified majority voting in the council. It also laid the foundations for the Common Foreign and Security Policy, which we are still struggling to achieve today. Now you may wonder why my party now denounces the very idea of a Common Foreign and Security Policy, when the original commitment, made in 1985, was actually founded upon the text of a draft treaty on that subject handed by Margaret Thatcher personally to Helmut Kohl at Chequers a few months before. I think the idea has had a long legitimacy, even if we haven't yet actually achieved it.

For a long time, in our European relationship as well as in our transatlantic one, Margaret Thatcher and I were quite clear on our political objectives, our personal relations were still compatible and the professionalism was equally well established. The decline in our European relationship started to set in early in 1989.

The pattern of those early years was described by Margaret in *The Downing Street Years*, the first written volume of her memoirs, as follows: 'As usual before European Councils, I held a number of preparatory meetings with Ministers and officials to ensure that I was properly briefed and to sort out with colleagues our precise objectives on each issue.'[13] It's true, that's what happened for a number of years.

In her own book, she's describing what she did before the Athens summit of December 1983. It continued like that for a number of years thereafter.

By the time we come to 1989 and the Madrid summit, which preceded Nigel Lawson's resignation, and later my own, that pattern of political partnership was falling apart. Policy was being clarified, not by discussion between ministers, but by officials bargaining and haggling over competitive speech drafts. The relationship between us had become distant. That's no way of achieving political coherence and unity. When, before the Madrid summit in June 1989, Nigel Lawson, the Chancellor of the Exchequer, and I suggested that we ought to have a meeting with the Prime Minister to discuss our handling of that meeting, we were denounced for having 'mounted an ambush' and 'organised a cabal'.[14] That was the sadness of the deteriorating relationship.

I wonder whether anything could have been done to prevent that deterioration. There were several factors that, in retrospect, might have made a difference. One, which is an interesting one, is that a man who'd held the ship together for a long time in Downing Street was the present Lord Williamson, who was the Cabinet deputy secretary with responsibility for co-ordination of our European policy. He was an ideal candidate to become the first non-French Secretary General of the European Commission, and we decided that we would like to get that job for a Briton and that David Williamson was the right man for it. We put him forward for that job and he succeeded Emile Noel, the first and until then the only holder of that important office. But did we, in winning that position in Brussels, lose the key man who could have held together our European partnership, which had served us well that far? I don't know.

One other tragic event, which preceded by not very long my ultimate departure from government, was the murder by the IRA of my oldest political friend – who also was one of Margaret Thatcher's closest associates, who had been her first, remarkably successful, parliamentary private secretary, Ian Gow. He was murdered, on 30 July 1990, by a bomb in his car outside his home. He was the political intimate of both Margaret and myself, and if anyone had provided the glue in our relationship when the going was rough, it had been him.

What are the crucial determinants of governmental success? Above all the common will of senior ministers to reach policy agreement clearly, plainly and effectively. That is the fundamental necessity. That may be made easier, may only be made possible in some cases, by the existence of a well-lubricated professional machine. But it cannot bridge an unbridgeable gap and the process may be rendered impossible by the lack of the personal relationship that is necessary. *Au fond* it is that personal political relationship that makes government tick and work – above all between the Prime Minister and his or her two senior colleagues, at the Foreign Office and the Treasury.

By the close of my partnership with Margaret Thatcher, the essential components of a successful political relationship had entirely disintegrated. The differences in personality, which had once successfully complemented each other, had become increasingly divisive. The professionalism of officialdom could no longer play a decisive part, when arrangements for regular liaison had never been properly established. And our political views of Britain's European destiny had grown ever further apart.

'The tragic conflict of loyalty, with which I wrestled for perhaps too long' – deep personal loyalty to the Prime Minister herself and equally powerful loyalty to the national interest – finally provoked the dissolution of our fifteen-year-old political partnership. The history of the marriage deserves much more attention than the story of the divorce.

The Rt Hon. the Lord Hurd of Westwell CH CBE PC

Foreign Secretary October 1989–July 1995

'After Iraq – what future for humanitarian intervention?'

Based on a lecture given at the London School of Economics and Political Science, 11 November 2003

The first year of my time as Foreign Secretary was filled with amazing good news. Within weeks the Berlin Wall came down and communist regimes began to collapse across Europe. The Cold War ended triumphantly for the West. This cheerful rhythm was broken when Saddam Hussein's seizure of Kuwait led inexorably to the Gulf War of 1991.

Throughout this time the processes of thought and action required of the British Foreign Secretary seemed straightforward. True, I had a prolonged tussle, only half behind the scenes, with the Prime Minister, Margaret Thatcher, on German unification. She drew back from outright opposition just in time to save us from falling over a cliff. But there seemed to me no particular moral or intellectual difficulty about any of this. On Germany we were trying, in the end successfully, to guide the Prime Minister back onto the track of a well-established foreign policy objective. In the Gulf War the War Cabinet had to take difficult and dangerous decisions; but here again the decision that Saddam Hussein's aggression had to be reversed required little argument, and the leadership which we received from President George Bush Senior was calm, reasonable and firm.

But towards the end of 1991 the disintegration of Yugoslavia, and the wars which followed in Croatia and then Bosnia, led us into a tangled thicket without paths or signposts. I do not want to go into the detail here. In my memoirs I try to set out as plainly as I can what we did, what we didn't do and why we acted or refrained.[1] There were indeed those who thought they saw clear signposts. Some believed this was Serb aggression and nothing else, not in essence different from the aggression which we had reversed in the Gulf War. Others, a majority in the Cabinet and the Commons, saw these as essentially civil wars where there was no clear British interest to justify us in taking risks. Neither analysis seemed adequate to the three British ministers, John Major, Malcolm Rifkind and myself, who shared the daily responsibility for making policy. Both at the time and in retrospect we were dissatisfied with the way in which we sailed these uncharted waters. We did not at the time philosophise because it was not that kind of crisis, but we were in effect exploring unhappily the doctrine of humanitarian intervention. To what extent was it the right or the duty of the international community in general, and Britain in particular, to send troops to kill and be killed in a country where Britain had no substantial commercial or strategic interest, but where Bosnian Serbs and to a lesser extent Bosnian Croats, and even on occasion Bosnian Muslims, were savagely wrecking each other's lives? The analysis of the British and French occasionally differed from that of the United States, thus creating turbulence within the alliance, which we managed, though sometimes with difficulty, to keep within limits.

I would like to examine the evolution since then of the doctrine of humanitarian intervention and the troubled nature of relationships among allies and within the UN which can result.

The concept of intervention on humanitarian grounds in the affairs of other countries has of course been around a long time. It underlay the efforts led by the Royal Navy to stamp out the slave trade in the nineteenth century. John Stuart Mill puzzled over the question when the Hapsburg Empire repressed revolts amongst its subjects in Hungary and Italy. During the early part of my time as Foreign Secretary the most striking example of humanitarian intervention was the initiative of the British Prime Minister, John Major, in 1991, as a result of which the Europeans and Americans went to the help of the Kurds in north Iraq. This was a relatively straightforward and successful enterprise. Our intervention in Bosnia was by contrast gradual and tentative. It began with economic aid, which was followed by the despatch of troops to protect the aid, which was followed by strenuous efforts by our military commanders on the ground to achieve pacification through local ceasefires and safe areas. These military efforts matched the simultaneous diplomatic efforts on a wider scale by our representatives including Lord Carrington, Cyrus Vance[2] and Lord Owen. As the war dragged miserably on the allied powers were galvanised into increasing their military strength on the ground and into greater use of NATO bombing. But throughout the aim of this use of force was not the imposition through bombs and missiles of a particular solution, let alone regime change in any of the capitals concerned. Throughout the aim was to curb atrocities and bring about a negotiated settlement.

After Bosnia, and the failure to intervene from outside to check the genocide in Rwanda, humanitarian intervention was placed much higher on the international agenda. There followed the rapid interventions in Kosovo, East Timor and Sierra Leone. The circumstances in each case were different, but the humanitarian motive was dominant. International law seemed to be evolving quite fast. No international treaty had established that it was legitimate for states to intervene for humanitarian purposes in the internal affairs of another state. Indeed, so far as there was a text on this matter it ran in the opposite direction. Article 2(7) of the UN Charter forbids the UN to intervene 'in matters which are essentially within the domestic jurisdiction of any State'. Forty years ago, when I worked as a junior member of the British delegation to the UN, this text was sacred. The UN had just been increased by a big inflow of new members, most of whom had recently gained their independence from colonial rule. They were proud and jealous of this independence, and deeply suspicious of any pretext which might lead their former colonial masters or anybody else to intervene in the way they ran their countries. But in 1998 Kofi Annan, Secretary General of the UN, gave a notable lecture on intervention at Ditchley.[3] 'State frontiers', he said, 'should no longer be seen as a watertight protection for war criminals or mass murderers. The fact that a conflict is "internal" does not give the parties any right to disregard the most basic rules of human conduct.' Looking ahead to the unfolding disaster in Kosovo he indicated that, if peaceful means failed, force might be needed. A little later, at the time of Kosovo, Tony Blair set out in Chicago his own considered analysis.[4] He said that we were witnessing the beginnings of a new doctrine of international community. The principle of non-interference should be qualified in important respects. Acts of genocide could never be a purely internal matter. Oppression which produced massive flows of refugees could properly be described as a 'threat to international peace and security'. Mr Blair quoted with approval one of President Kennedy's more eloquent but less meaningful phrases: 'freedom is indivisible and when one man is enslaved who is free?'

There is no mystery as to how this general change in attitude summarised by the Secretary General and the Prime Minister had come about. Public opinion in the Western democracies was no longer prepared to accept that their governments were powerless to prevent man-made atrocities on a large scale when these atrocities were brought to their attention regularly by the mass media. Two questions were not seriously tested. To what extent did countries outside the family of Western democracies share this view? And what level of cost in terms of lives and money were the Western democracies ready to incur in the effort for peace with justice?

But I wrote at the time in a book called *The Search for Peace*: 'We are all interventionists now.'[5] That was written in 1997. I am not so sure now. Political doctrine and indeed international law evolve, not so much through discussion as through practical demonstration. Events since September 11 2001 have to some extent reopened the discussion. The tragedy of September 11 moved the international debate away from the problems of humanitarian intervention back to the much more traditional emphasis on self-defence. Self-defence has always been accepted, for example in Article 51 of the [UN] Charter, as a proper ground for military action. The campaign in Afghanistan was justified and generally accepted by world opinion as an exercise of self-defence, given that there was no doubt that the authors of the attacks on

September 11 had their hiding place in Afghanistan, and were protected by the Afghan government.

A familiar discussion about failed states was resumed, but with a difference. The failure of Somalia, for example, was after September 11 analysed not in terms of the hardship for Somalis, but rather as a dangerous opportunity for terrorists to establish a new base to attack the West.

The primary argument for the Anglo-American pre-emptive strike against Iraq was also self-defence. In the United States, though not, fortunately, in the United Kingdom, a short-lived attempt was made to link Saddam Hussein directly with Al-Qaeda and thus with September 11. The absence of hard evidence for this allegation caused it to evaporate. There remained a stronger argument based not on September 11 but on Saddam Hussein's record as an aggressor and his undoubted possession in earlier years of weapons of mass destruction. But this argument too evaporated as a result of the failure to discover the weapons which it was argued were such a threat to Iraq's neighbours and to all of us.

Weaker supplementary arguments, still based on self-defence, were then produced, for example that the threat came not from actual weapons but from plans once again to possess such weapons. Or else it was maintained that Saddam's defiance of Security Council resolutions stretching back to the Gulf War of 1991 justified an attack on him. The difficulty about these extensions of the self-defence argument was that they in no way justified an immediate pre-emptive strike based on the American military timetable. They pointed instead towards the policy preferred by the Secretary General and the majority of the Security Council, namely sustained peaceful pressure on the regime and renewal of UN inspections, rather than the despatch of an army to kill and be killed. In his lecture to Justice, Lord Alexander of Weedon neatly demolished the arguments apparently used by the Attorney General in upholding the legality of the Anglo-American pre-emptive strike.[6]

The virtual collapse of a justification based on self-defence for the attack on Iraq led to a sharp switch back to the humanitarian argument. The Prime Minister has always found himself most at home with that argument – namely that whatever the truth about weapons, Saddam Hussein was an evil ruler and that Iraq and the world are better off without him. Put simply like that, the statement cannot be denied. There can be no serious questioning of the evil nature of his regime or of the great harm he did to his own people and their neighbours. But such simplicity is not of this world. In the real world two further questions fall to be answered – the question of *authority* and the question of *aftermath*.

Who is to decide that a ruler is so evil that on humanitarian grounds it is right to go to war to remove him? 'Regime change' is a tidy antiseptic phrase. It has involved in this case, in addition to our own mounting casualties, killing a much larger number of innocent Iraqis and wrecking a country already badly damaged by sanctions and a ruthless dictatorship. So much was predictable. But who is to weigh the merits of this action against the advantage of removing that dictator? The answer is clear in the UN Charter.

According to the charter this judgement cannot be left to those who plan a war, but it is reserved to the Security Council. In the case of Kosovo we went to war on humanitarian grounds without achieving such a judgement from the Security Council. We made no attempt in the Security Council because we thought it likely that Russia would veto the resolution. In 2003 the situation was different. Before the Iraq war the Prime Minister persuaded the President of the United States that we should try to obtain specific authorisation from the Security Council for the use of force. We tried, and we failed. Looking back we can see how feeble it was in the heat of our disappointment to try to blame this failure on the French. The full weight of our diplomacy was brought to bear on the elected members of the council. It was not French lobbying or the threat of a French veto which caused these governments to resist us. For good reason or bad, they believed that what we were asking was unreasonable and unacceptable to their own peoples. Yet we went ahead and started a war.

Having served four years in the British mission to the UN, I have no illusions about the shortcomings of the Security Council. It is certainly not a gathering of democrats. The veto reflects the power structures of 1945, not today, and has been used, particularly in the past by the Soviet Union and more recently by the United States, for reasons far removed from their own essential interests. There is a strong case for enlarging the council and for modifying the veto, and there are plenty of plans for both. But the plans gather dust; neither in practice is going to come about in the foreseeable future.

But it does not follow that because the Security Council is flawed we should go back to the jungle and believe that we, because of our strong right arm (or that of the superpower), are the only valid judges in authorising war.

That is why the Secretary General, in his cautious persuasive way, confronted member states with the problem of authority when he spoke to the General Assembly on 23 September 2003. Kofi Annan said:

> According to this argument [justifying pre-emptive force] states are not obliged to wait until there is agreement in the Security Council. Instead they reserve the right to act unilaterally or in ad hoc coalitions. This logic represents a fundamental challenge to the principles on which, however imperfectly, world peace and stability have rested for the last fifty-eight years. My concern is that if it were to be adopted it could set precedents that resulted in the proliferation of the unilateral and lawless use of force with or without justification.

He went on to urge member states to discuss how in these circumstances the UN could best respond to massive violations of human rights. He asked whether the UN should for the first time discuss criteria for early pre-emptive action in such cases.

In his address to Chatham House on 14 October 2003, the Archbishop of Canterbury suggested setting up a body of wise and

respected persons from across the world to weigh such cases –
presumably in an advisory role to the Security Council, but possessing
a personal and collective authority which could strongly influence its
deliberations. Another possibility would be to place more weight on the
role of the Secretary General himself. It is characteristic of Kofi Annan
that he did not suggest this himself, possibly remembering the
difficulties which his predecessor Dag Hammarskjöld ran into when he
tried to elevate Article 99 of the charter into giving the Secretary
General an almost priestly authority.

These are ideas not yet acted on. The question of authority for such
a pre-emptive strike remains unsettled. Yet quite apart from questions
of ethics and legality it is clear now that action without authority can
add substantially to the difficulties of those who take it.

This leads to the question of *aftermath*. Obviously the case for
humanitarian intervention does not rest simply on the arguments for
removing an evil ruler. There must be a calculation that the regime
which follows is not only better but matches at least to some extent
the ideals of freedom and democracy which we often proclaim and
which are embodied in the various international declarations on
human rights and indeed in the charter itself. The toppling of statues
is not enough. Nor is the putting on trial of the dictator concerned.
What counts is what follows.

The debate on humanitarian intervention in the early nineties had
failed to cope adequately with aftermath. It concentrated on how you
get in, not on what followed, or how you get out.

In Bosnia, Kosovo and East Timor what followed was a small-scale
exercise in benevolent imperialism, which in Bosnia and Kosovo
continues to this day, still relying on the presence of foreign troops. In
Afghanistan a skilful political exercise put in power a distinguished
president, but not yet a central government capable of asserting
authority over the outlying provinces or preventing the limited revival
of the Taliban. In Iraq what followed a brilliant military campaign was
a mess – a mess characterised by looting, lawless streets and now a

resistance movement which resorts to terrorism. The Anglo-Americans as the occupying power assumed responsibilities for law and order which to a large extent they retain. They have failed to discharge these responsibilities in Baghdad and in the centre of the country. The post-war plan was based on assumptions in the Pentagon which quickly proved false. They ignored their own ignorance and trusted advisers who others knew were untrustworthy. The British government subordinated its thinking so completely to the United States that no serious questions were asked about that plan and no attempt made to modify it in the light of British experience in Iraq or the Middle East. No attention was paid to those who predicted correctly that while most Iraqis would rejoice at Saddam Hussein's overthrow, it did not follow that they would welcome foreign military occupation.

The recklessness of these assumptions in the Pentagon passes belief. So does the failure of Britain to question them. To the extent that our newspapers still cover Iraq (the coverage is now puny compared to that in America) they focus on President Bush's growing political difficulty. But our own Prime Minister was equally involved in the same gamble.

It would be a disaster, not just for Britain and America and Iraq but for the whole world, if Iraq descended into anarchy. The resistance movement in parts of the country gains recruits from the shootings, arrests, searches and checkpoints which are the inevitable consequences of military occupation. To take an example: when the Americans shot eighteen Iraqis in the streets of Falluja and followed it up by killing eight friendly Iraqi policemen, you did not have to wheel in Al-Qaeda, or shadowy Syrians or the phantom of Saddam Hussein, to explain the town's hostility to American occupation. The resistance and its terrorist method will never have the strength to dislodge the occupying armies. Vietnam is no parallel; but unless the present pattern can be changed, the resistance can frustrate a peaceful political outcome. The real comparison is not with Vietnam but with Palestine or Chechnya. Personally I find that formidable enough.

Immediate withdrawal of British and American troops is obviously unthinkable. The efforts now being made to build up Iraqi security forces and to move towards an Iraqi constitution and the transfer of sovereignty to a decent Iraqi authority must be right and supported by everybody. But agreement now on the only possible way forward in Iraq should not blind us to the lessons which need to be learnt from the past. The notion that our invasion would create a model Western-style democracy, plus a free market economy as advocated by the *Wall Street Journal*, plus a foreign policy which quickly recognised Israel, was always unreal and presumptuous, and is now defunct. Certainly the Arab world is held back by the absence of free institutions and a civil society. But this gap cannot be filled by Cruise missiles and military occupation. We can help from outside, but the Arabs have to plant institutions in their own soil – as is beginning to happen, albeit slowly, along the Gulf, including even Saudi Arabia, and will have to happen in Egypt.

Some of the lessons we are learning may be beneficial. For example, it is clear the United States needs partners if it is to follow its own constructive instincts. The armed forces of the United States need to be trained for the previously despised task of nation-building. It is also clear that the greatest single international asset which Britain now possesses is the professionalism of our armed forces, even though our politicians may make improper use of it in pursuit of ill-considered policies.

The fundamental lesson, I believe, lies in better understanding the necessary relationship between the United States and her allies. In this respect Iraq is not a model to be followed but an example to be avoided. We British should understand that in the penny-farthing relationship which we now have with the United States the farthing is gradually getting smaller. Despite the Prime Minister's skill and total loyalty to the United States, events in Iraq have shown the limits of loyalty's reward. We know now from his experience that a British government cannot realistically expect to exercise the kind of influence over United States policy as was enjoyed by Winston Churchill or Margaret

Thatcher, though even then both of these knew that they represented the junior partner. There is only one remedy for this imbalance and it lies in Europe. The Anglo-American alliance remains valuable, but by itself is no longer a proper basis for a vigorous and effective British foreign policy. We Europeans should not wish to set ourselves up as rivals to the United States or pretend that we can do so even if we wished. It is only by a valid partnership between the United States and a Europe which works together that we can in practice tackle these problems of authority and aftermath in any future humanitarian intervention. This requires a galvanising of the European diplomatic and military effort. In such a co-operative effort Britain is at least an equal party with any other European state. It is odd that those who oppose such a European effort on grounds of loss of sovereignty are prepared to accept the much greater subordination to the United States which we now see in Iraq.

It may be applied more cautiously in future but the doctrine of humanitarian intervention is certainly not defunct. Although the searchlight of the modern media plays erratically on the world, leaving many terrible events in darkness, it can light up a scene of man-made horror with such intensity that inaction becomes indefensible. Realists should not mock the idealism which then demands action, for it is sincere and deeply rooted. But the two problems of authority and aftermath are not just theoretical concepts to be tossed about in debate. There is no precise remedy which will fit all cases. But recent events show that the involvement of the UN, with all its faults, is indispensable. Without some form of UN legitimacy a major armed intervention is likely to run into trouble; without access to UN skills and resources nation-building is unlikely to thrive.

In my memoirs I describe the Suez crisis of 1956 from the insignificant viewpoint of a young British diplomat to the UN.[7] I remember well the scorn heaped on the UN in Britain during those weeks when we were preparing to use our own right arm to remove what we believed to be a desperate threat to our economy and our security, namely Nasser's nationalisation of the canal. Yet when the crunch came we were forced back to the UN for the remedy, in the form of the UN force rapidly assembled by Dag Hammarskjöld and Lester Pearson. The parallel is far from exact, but the same scorn for the UN was certainly there in the US as they planned their pre-emptive strike on Iraq. Great powers are not penitent by nature. It will be enough if the US and Britain, like Britain and France in 1956, are forced to accept for the future that there is an international community, that it is embodied, however imperfectly, in the UN, and that the support or opposition of the UN must weigh heavily in the scales of any military intervention which is not strictly and clearly in self-defence.

Sir Malcolm Rifkind KCMG QC MP

Foreign Secretary July 1995–May 1997

'The Special Relationship between the United States and
the United Kingdom – is it special?'

Based on a lecture given at the London School of Economics
and Political Science, 18 November 2003

The job of Foreign Secretary has, of course, changed much over the years. Sir Edward Grey was Foreign Secretary from 1905 to 1916. For the greater part of that time, he never left the shores of the United Kingdom but dealt with his global and imperial responsibilities from his desk in King Charles Street. Modern foreign ministers are not so fortunate, either in this country or elsewhere. Hans-Dietrich Genscher, who was a long-serving foreign minister of West Germany, used to travel so much around the world that the question was asked: 'What is the difference between God and Genscher?' The answer was: 'God is everywhere. Genscher is everywhere except Germany.'

Foreign ministers are unusual as politicians. They rarely have the opportunity to initiate a major new policy, see it through and bring it to a successful conclusion. International affairs began before they assumed office, and will continue after they have left it. Each is only one of many players on the international field. The business of conducting foreign policy is more like a conveyor belt than a ladder. The great Marquis of Salisbury once remarked:

> There is nothing dramatic in the success of a diplomatist. His victories are made up of a series of microscopic advantages: of a judicious suggestion here, of an opportune civility there, of a wise concession at one moment, and a far-sighted persistence at another; of sleepless tact, immovable calmness and patience that no folly, no provocation, no blunder can shake.

These are special qualities. It is by no means certain that those invited to serve as Foreign Secretary have them. Appointments can be for the most unlikely of reasons: Stanley Baldwin, having ruled out Austen Chamberlain and Lord Halifax as his Foreign Secretary, apparently said to Anthony Eden, 'It looks as if it will have to be you.'

This chapter will consider the Special Relationship between the United States and the United Kingdom, itself an example of the seamless web of historical development that has seen both constancy and change over a long period of years.[1]

In our time, we have been used to thinking of the United States as the world superpower. In any relationship with the United Kingdom, the Americans are, necessarily, seen as by far the senior partner. It is worth remembering, however, that for all of the nineteenth century, and for at least the early part of the twentieth, it was the other way round. The British Empire was the world power that mattered in most of Asia, in Africa, and on the high seas.

The United States was extending its influence inexorably, and its late intervention in the First World War helped ensure German defeat. But isolationism followed, and until Roosevelt's day, American power was most exercised in the Pacific, in Latin America and in the Far East.

It is also ironic to recall that at its birth and for a period thereafter, the closest ally of the United States was France, whereas Britain was, for obvious reasons, the enemy. The changing nature of the American–British–French relationship is one of the great joys of the last two centuries. It is not just the United States and France that have had a difficult and testing relationship. Britain and France have hardly fared better. On one occasion, Palmerston was visited by the French ambassador, who in trying to please his host remarked that if he had not been born a Frenchman, he would have liked to have been born an Englishman, to which Palmerston is reputed to have replied, 'How interesting. If I had not been born an Englishman, I would have liked to have been born an Englishman.' To which, as a Scot, I have to say, 'Och man, have you got no ambition?'

There is a misconception that the American interest in Britain and in Europe as a whole was as a result of the Second World War, and of the subsequent need to contain the Soviet Union and the threat of communism. According to this theory, with the end of that threat, and the victory of capitalism over communism, America will lose its interest in Europe and revert to a preoccupation with the Pacific and the Far East. Like all such theories, this one cannot be completely repudiated, but it is fundamentally unsound. It is worth recollecting that the American physical presence in Europe did not begin in the Second World War in the battle against Hitler, but in 1917, with the need to defeat the Kaiser. Throughout the twentieth century, the United States, albeit after significant hesitation, has always concluded that the security and freedom of Europe was crucial to its own strategic interests, and reacted accordingly.

Because of Britain's unique position after the fall of France, and as a consequence of the personal relationship forged between Winston Churchill and Franklin Roosevelt, the Second World War became the paramount example of Anglo-American co-operation and common interest. Of course, Roosevelt and Churchill disagreed on many issues, but on the fundamentals they were as one, and their common purpose never wavered.

This co-operation continued in the necessary work that had to be done after 1945 and the fall of Hitler. The change of government in the United Kingdom, with Attlee's victory, did not change the fundamental relationship any more than did Truman's succession to Roosevelt. Ernest Bevin was a close ally of the Americans in the founding of the United Nations, the establishment of NATO and the building of the post-Second World War order.

But the United States was more perceptive than the British as to the implications of the massive weakening of the British Empire and of its inexorable decline. This came to a head with the Suez crisis in 1956. British influence in the Middle East and throughout the world collapsed after the Suez crisis, when Britain and France, in secret collusion with Israel, tried to destroy Gamal Abdul Nasser, but were forced to withdraw by a hostile and uncompromising United States.

This is a good moment to be reminded that at that time, unilateral military action against an Arab state so incensed Washington that they threatened economic sanctions against Britain at the United Nations. It is often forgotten that Suez was the first time that Britain exercised its right of veto in the Security Council. But although the UN could be blocked, London was unable to stop the drain on our gold reserves, instigated by the Americans, and Eisenhower refused to help until the military action was suspended.

Why were the Americans so hostile? After all, the British were only trying to exercise regime change against an Arab dictator, who had flouted his international obligations, and was a threat to the security of his neighbours. In part, it was because the Americans liked to think of themselves, at that time, as the natural friend of the Third World, and as the first nation to be decolonised from the British Empire. They were more interested in the Pacific Canal than the Suez Canal, and felt that they could afford to be high minded.

In later years, both Eisenhower and his former Secretary of State, John Foster Dulles, admitted that they had been wrong to force the British and French to withdraw. The result had been the collapse of British influence, to the benefit of the Soviets, a triumph for Nasser and the destabilisation of moderate Arab regimes. One consequence was the violent overthrow of the Hashemite monarchy in Iraq in 1958, which led in due course to the rise of Saddam Hussein.

Suez was a severe blow for Anglo-American relations, but it is remarkable and significant how quickly these relations were repaired. Harold Macmillan took it as a prime objective of his Prime Ministership to achieve such an end, and the healthy relationship he created with President Kennedy led to the Bermuda summit and the agreement by the United States on providing the United Kingdom, through Polaris, with its nuclear deterrent. Such a transformation in the years after Suez was not simply as a result of British desire to repair the frayed relationship. It was also because the Americans, at the height of the Cold War, needed to re-establish closest possible co-operation with their main European ally.

One should not underestimate the degree of intimacy which the older Macmillan achieved with the young John F. Kennedy. Indeed, during the 1961 Bermuda summit, Kennedy felt so relaxed in Macmillan's presence that he confided to him that if he, Kennedy, did not have a woman every three days, he would have a terrible headache. It is not known what Harold Macmillan thought of this revelation. On the other hand, Macmillan had been known to remark with his usual ambiguity, 'Whenever I feel bored, I like to go to bed with a Trollope.'

So much for the historical background. It is worth exploring what are the strengths and weaknesses of the American–British relationship. The strengths are very significant, and continue to be highly relevant. First of all, the United Kingdom is not only a European state and a member of the European Union. By virtue of its geography as well as its history and culture, it is also an Atlantic power. There is no necessary conflict between these two aspects of its identity, nor does a choice have to be made, as is so often implied by those arguing from either the European or the Atlanticist perspective. Indeed, the United States has a comparable dual identity, being both an Atlantic and a Pacific nation.

Secondly, the Anglo-Saxon background and common English language remain of profound importance to the relationship. They not only provide an ease of communication and a natural, informal empathy that transcends language difficulties; there is also a shared historical perspective, which has developed over several centuries.

Thirdly, the United Kingdom, having been a superpower and having retained a significant military capability, attaches far more importance than most European countries to the use of military force as a complement to diplomatic pressure in the resolution of international difficulties. Like the United States, Britain finds no difficulty in subscribing to Frederick the Great's dictum that 'diplomacy without arms is like music without instruments'. Of course, France is also a significant military power but that has not led to any French empathy with American diplomatic and political objectives since the days of Charles de Gaulle.

The United Kingdom is also, of course, an important ally for the

United States because of its other global roles. Britain remains a permanent member of the Security Council, with a veto. It is a nuclear power; it is the leading member of the Commonwealth, which brings together nations from every continent and is an important forum for dialogue. It is still the world's fourth largest economy. The cumulative effect of all these considerations is that the United Kingdom, although much junior to America, is an ally worth having.

But there must also be acknowledged the substantial and unavoidable weaknesses in the relationship. Inevitably, the most important is the disparity of size and power. Britain may be the most significant military force in the world after the United States, but it is a very long way behind the United States, as we have seen in both Gulf Wars. America is often interested by Britain's opinions, and is prepared to defer to them when its own vital interests are not at stake, but, as we have seen in the recent past, the United States having reached a conclusion as to its policy will not change it simply because of British disagreement.

It is also true that although the end of the Cold War has not removed the United States' interest in the stability of Europe, that objective now has to be shared, more substantially, with other concerns that the Americans have, which are of less importance either to Britain or to Europe as a whole. The problems of North Korea, China and Latin America can never be ignored by any American government, and with the Cold War behind them, and with Britain neither willing nor able to make an immediate contribution to those more distant regions, that has its impact on the intensity of the relationship. Thus the relationship provides mutual benefits.

The President and the Prime Minister could not be closer. But why is public support in Britain more fragile than it has been for years? Tony Blair is far from being the first British Prime Minister to attach great importance to his relationship with the American President. Why, therefore, is he the first to be lampooned, regularly, as the President's poodle? It is a fate that Margaret Thatcher never suffered despite her long and intimate alliance with Ronald Reagan.

The reason is not that difficult to find. Thatcher was perfectly willing to swing her handbag at the Americans if she judged that British interests required it. There is, as yet, no evidence that Blair would even wag his finger in public, whatever he might be saying in private.

Few of us would disagree with any British Prime Minister who makes the relationship with Washington and the White House a central part of his foreign policy. The British are more interested in power than philosophy; more concerned with influence than ideology. The Americans have that power. We want to have the influence. So Lloyd George cultivated Woodrow Wilson, Churchill was close to Roosevelt, Macmillan charmed Kennedy and Thatcher lectured Bush Senior. Blair is part of that tradition and we can welcome that. But that is where the similarity ends.

Blair's support for George Bush seems to be unconditional and unqualified, particularly in regard to the Iraq war. But what about his pressure for a second UN resolution? What about his support for UN involvement in Iraqi reconstruction? What about his promotion of the Middle East road map? Surely these have all been policies that have begun in London, and for which Blair can take the credit?

That is all true but with a fairly fundamental qualification. Yes, the Foreign Office worked night and day with splendid British initiatives. And, yes, some of them were taken up by the Americans. But the whole point is that whenever the Americans don't like them, Blair doesn't growl defiance.

If you think I am being unfair, just ponder on the following. Blair told us that the invasion of Iraq and the military overthrow of Saddam Hussein was a great moral and ethical imperative. Well if it was, why wasn't it for the first five years of his Prime Ministership? The truth is that Blair had not the slightest intention of advocating regime change in Iraq until Bush told him it had become American policy. Likewise, the British public were told that a second UN resolution was essential until it became obvious that it wasn't going to happen. Then we were told by Blair that if a second resolution wasn't achieved because of one unreasonable veto, that could be ignored. In the event the problem was not one veto but the absence of even a bare majority of the Security Council in favour of immediate attack.

George Bush wasn't guilty of such evasion and deliberate ambiguity. He had made it crystal clear from the beginning that the Americans would attack with or without international support. Blair started by insisting on the UN route but when Bush came to shove he crumbled quickly.

Previous Prime Ministers have been quite prepared to fight it out with the Americans if necessary. Churchill did not hide his concern that Roosevelt was too trusting of Stalin. Harold Wilson refused to send British troops to Vietnam. Thatcher roundly condemned the Americans for the invasion of Grenada. Indeed, at the height of that crisis Thatcher gave a remarkable interview on the BBC World Service. She declared:

> We in the Western countries, the Western democracies, use our force to defend our way of life. We do not use it to walk into other people's countries, independent sovereign territories . . . If you are pronouncing a new law that wherever communism reigns against the will of the people . . . there the United States shall enter, we are going to have really terrible wars in the world.

She was also bitterly critical of US attempts to impose sanctions on British firms like John Brown Engineering, which had won contracts for the Soviet gas pipeline during the Cold War.

During that latter spat I was sent by Thatcher and Howe to Washington to try and reach a compromise with the American deputy Secretary of State, Kenneth Dam. We did. The only thing we couldn't agree on was whether to call the compromise the Rifkind–Dam agreement or, as the Americans preferred, the Dam–Rifkind agreement. These disagreements did nothing to reduce Ronald Reagan's regard for the British Prime Minister.

When the war in Bosnia first erupted neither the Americans nor the

Europeans considered it a serious threat to European security or to their respective national interests. If we, or they, had done, we would have reacted as with the Iraqi invasion of Kuwait or the attack on the World Trade Center. There would have been a commitment to use whatever military or other means were necessary to ensure a satisfactory resolution of the crisis.

The issue, at the time, was whether we should be involved at all, other than through traditional diplomacy. The Americans decided against. The British and other Europeans decided that military support for humanitarian convoys was essential if there was not to be a huge, unnecessary civilian loss of life. The result was UNPROFOR with a large military contribution from the United Kingdom. It was John Major and Douglas Hurd who pushed this through a British Cabinet that did not want Britain to be militarily involved at all.

It was always open to the Bosnian government to have withdrawn approval for the presence of UNPROFOR in their territory. If they had done so, at any time, UNPROFOR would have had no choice but to withdraw. It would then have been possible for the Americans to implement their 'lift and strike' policy, of lifting the arms embargo and launching air strikes against the Bosnian Serbs, without any need for British, French or other approval. The fact that this never occurred is conclusive that the Bosnian government attached more importance to the continuation of UNPROFOR than to the possible benefits of 'lift and strike' using US air power.

The US Congress refused to allow a single US soldier on the ground in Bosnia while calling for effective action against the Serbs. This resulted in the 'dual key' policy, requiring American and European agreement before any use of air power, which was highly unsatisfactory but which was inevitable as long as the country doing the bombing had no forces on the ground, while the countries with forces on the ground were liable both to be bombed by mistake or to be subject to retaliatory action by the Bosnian Serbs. One only has to ask whether the Americans would ever have allowed the reverse to apply, with only US troops on the ground and Europeans carrying out bombing, without a dual key.

There have been recent allegations by armchair polemicists that great damage was done to NATO and US–British relations by our policy on Bosnia. I am, of course, aware that there was much criticism but NATO and US–British relations remained robust throughout because both governments were determined that they would. For example, at the height of the Bosnian crisis, when we were in disagreement with Washington, I asked Bill Perry, the US Defence Secretary, if the US would sell Cruise missiles to the UK. Within days I received a positive response combined only with a concern that any public statements by us should not lead any other country to assume that the US would sell Cruise missiles to them. British support to the US in Iraq and Libya was far more important to Washington than our real disagreements over Bosnia. Indeed, in his recent memoirs Douglas Hurd has revealed that in the middle of the Bosnian crisis the Americans tried to persuade him to become Secretary General of NATO.[2] So much for the argument that British policy on Bosnia severely damaged the Special Relationship with Washington.

I have concentrated, so far, on these several occasions, when British Prime Ministers made no secret of their deep disagreement with US policy, in order to demonstrate that the health and vitality of the Special Relationship does not depend on British obedience to the Americans. It is Mr Blair's failure to realise this that is in danger of leading to public disillusionment, in this country, with the alliance.

But, of course, the relationship could not have survived and prospered over many years if not only the British government but also British public opinion had not shared the values and the political priorities of the United States on most of the major issues that both countries had to deal with. Thus Britain, unlike most other European countries apart from France, maintained high defence budgets and strong military forces throughout the Cold War. British public opinion as well as successive Conservative and Labour governments repudiated unilateral disarmament and supported both Polaris and Trident, as well as the proposed deployment of Cruise and Pershing missiles.

Most people in Britain had no difficulty in our alliance with the United States during the first Gulf War; the Americans gave us steadfast support during the Falklands and we stood shoulder to shoulder with Washington during the war in Afghanistan to root out the Al-Qaeda terrorists. Likewise in Iraq, during the 1990s it was Britain that was closest to the United States in maintaining sanctions and enforcing the no-fly zone that was effective in emasculating Saddam Hussein and preventing him from attacking his neighbours.

Thus the Special Relationship has not just been based on sentiment and a shared Atlanticist identity but on common interests, common values and joint action.

What is the benefit of the relationship to the United States? It did not need military allies to defeat Saddam Hussein in either Gulf War but for both domestic and international reasons it preferred to have them. While we are often reminded of the US's tendency to go it alone, few American Presidents like doing so and American public opinion is often deeply disturbed when the United States acts alone. British support is particularly welcomed because she is seen as a strong, democratic ally, and Churchill, Thatcher and Blair have all achieved a resonance with the American public that no other European politicians have acquired in the last fifty years.

In addition Britain is a worthwhile ally on the Security Council; it can be a bridge to Europe, as when Blair co-ordinated Spanish, Italian and east European support for the recent Iraqi war; and its armed forces, while small compared to the Americans', are recognised to be of exceptional calibre, whether as special forces or as peacekeepers.

What about the value of the relationship to the United Kingdom? Clearly it is important to have more influence than almost anyone else with the world's only super-duper power. It is sometimes said that that is all very well but the Americans, once they have decided on their vital interests, will never change policy just to suit the British. That is true, but not just for the Americans. The British, for example, would have refused to acquiesce in the Argentine occupation of the Falklands even if the Americans had so wished. Neither country will budge when its vital interests are at stake. But on many issues the Americans are open to persuasion and Britain is more able to persuade them than most others.

The relationship has also had practical benefits for Britain, particularly in the defence and security field. No other country was provided with the Polaris or Trident systems. We were the first country to whom the Americans were willing to sell Cruise missiles. We have far greater access to US intelligence than any other country and we share ours with them. There is a political dialogue between the two countries which is far greater and much deeper than that which the US has with any other ally.

That relationship is now more important than ever. The greatest casualty of the recent Iraq war was Western unity. The deep differences between the United States and both France and Germany were bitter and have hardly begun to be resolved. There is a deep distrust between Washington and Paris, and distrust breeds misunderstanding and division. One is reminded of Metternich's alleged remark when he was told that the Russian ambassador had just died: 'Ah. I wonder what his motive can have been.'

Britain can be a bridge between the Americans and so-called old Europe. It is essential that Western and NATO unity is re-established as otherwise the battle against terrorism and nuclear proliferation will be far harder to win.

So my conclusion is that there *is* a special relationship. It is very much in the interests of both countries that it continues and it is in the interests of the wider world as well. But although Bush and Blair could not be closer friends and colleagues, the links between the two countries are under considerable strain because of a degree of disillusion in Britain. The main reason is the Iraq war, which has led to a deep feeling in the United Kingdom that we were misled and taken into war on an unjustifiable basis by both the President and the Prime Minister. To some extent that is now history and there is a strong common interest that the Americans and the British should not only leave Iraq but leave at least having established an opportunity for the Iraqis to enjoy the rule of law and representative government.

For the future Mr Blair must recognise two things. First, that if he wishes Britain to be a bridge between America and Europe that is all very well. But any bridge will be very unstable if it leans too much in one direction. Second, it will not be sufficient for him to make representations to the President, in private, whenever he believes that American policy is unwise or unsound. While that is the normal way in which close allies try to sort out their differences, the British public need to know that their Prime Minister will fight in public as well as in private whenever the public interest so requires. That he has not yet done and it is time that he did.

However, our relationship with the United States remains fundamentally sound and rightly so. Sometimes the Europeans get alarmed by American initiatives or unilateral actions. The British tend to be less worried. They remember Churchill's view that 'you can always rely on the Americans to do the right thing when they have tried every other option'.

Afterword: New Labour's Foreign Policy

Christopher Hill and Tim Oliver

The election of Tony Blair and New Labour in May 1997 came as no surprise either at home or abroad. The Conservative Party, in power for eighteen years, seemed exhausted of ideas and credibility. Rocked by scandals and divisions, most notably over Britain's relations with Europe, the Conservatives were easy prey to a New Labour party unified by a strong and young leader, and armed with a ruthless and energetic campaign machine, a fresh image and the language of globalisation. Yet despite this dynamic approach embracing a range of issues linked to the international arena, New Labour remained conspicuously quiet on the issue of foreign policy throughout the electoral campaign, as it had in opposition. So it was that as the end of the twentieth century approached Britain found herself with a new, more secure and confident government, but one that lacked both experience and a clear programme for how to direct the nation's foreign affairs.

Given such an unsure beginning, it might be considered surprising that in the years since 1997 New Labour has pursued such an active and at times deeply controversial foreign policy. Yet despite the talk of foreign policy with an 'ethical dimension', and 'Blair's [six] wars', there have also been significant elements of continuity with the foreign policies of previous governments.[1] Indeed, despite the criticisms which

Blair made of his immediate Conservative predecessors (who under John Major had been paralysed over the European Union and to some degree in the Balkans), it was evident that there was a wish to build on the foundations of Margaret Thatcher's revival of British confidence as a player in world politics.

This concluding chapter seeks to outline New Labour's foreign policies and to tie them into these longer-term trends. In doing so we pose three key questions. First, to what extent has New Labour changed British foreign policy, compared to what it inherited from the previous Conservative government, especially in the key area of the transatlantic relationship? Second, how do Blair's first two Foreign Secretaries, Robin Cook and Jack Straw, compare – especially in terms of their impact on events?[2] Finally, what interim judgement can be reached on the foreign policy legacy of New Labour and in particular of Blair?

Robin Cook 1997–2001

As the first Labour Foreign Secretary since 1979 Robin Cook was always going to face high expectations. During the 1990s he had developed a reputation for a piercing intellect and powerful oratorical skills, put to use most effectively in demolishing the case of the Conservative government after the 1996 Scott report, on the Iraqi supergun scandal. Seen by some as a custodian of the left in New Labour, he was, as Rhiannon Vickers has pointed out, certainly in the liberal internationalist tradition of the party.[3] In the 1970s and early 1980s he was, like many in the Labour Party, an active member of CND, as well as the author of a range of pamphlets covering issues such as NATO and the Cold War. He also campaigned for Britain to withdraw from the European Community.[4] Nonetheless, he also took part in expert discussions on the future of British foreign policy at Chatham House, and came to accept the importance of Britain's membership of what was to be the European Union. In office he was to become yet more positive towards the EU, and highly esteemed by his colleagues in the Council of Ministers.

Cook, along with Tony Blair, Gordon Brown, Peter Mandelson and Alastair Campbell, was a member of the core group that constructed New Labour. Yet Cook's tendency to work more on his own than to network left him precariously vulnerable to the Blair–Brown tensions that have shaped Labour politics both in opposition and in government. In particular, enduring difficulties with his fellow Scot Brown contributed to Cook being assigned to the foreign affairs portfolio. It kept him out of the domestic arena that Brown had defined as his own.[5] Combined with an election campaign that said little about foreign policy and a promise to establish the Department for International Development – thus depriving the Foreign and Commonwealth Office of the development portfolio – Cook might have been expected to begin his work as Foreign Secretary quietly. In practice, he was determined to make his mark, a product of his own ambitious ideas and the need to put Labour's endless travails with foreign policy to rest.

Cook set out his stall in his first days in office, being intent on remodelling both the style and the substance of the UK's external relations. He oversaw the launch of an FCO 'mission statement' and the founding of the left-leaning think tank the Foreign Policy Centre, welcomed new approaches to branding the UK's public diplomacy, and made clear his intention to open up the FCO to new ideas, people and ethnic groups. In so doing Cook seemed determined to make British foreign policy and the FCO more inclusive and progressive. As he noted when presenting the FCO mission statement:

> We live in a world in which nation states are interdependent. In that modern world foreign policy is not divorced from domestic policy but a central part of any political programme. In order to achieve our goals for the people of Britain we need a foreign strategy that supports the same goals.[6]

Such an approach worked in part because it aligned itself with Blair's developing foreign policy ideas; it stressed the nature of a Labour Party committed to the concept of an international society, to human rights and to development. By contrast the previous Conservative government was painted as Machiavellian and steeped in myopic realism. In short, it struck the right notes in many quarters, inside and outside the UK, with those who were frustrated with what they saw as a stagnant British foreign policy, not yet in tune with the country's economic recovery and cultural vibrancy. But was this a change of style more than substance?

To begin with the change seemed radical, while even Cook's enemies would not usually have seen him as favouring froth over policy. Yet he was soon to become hostage to one of his own publicity coups, as one idea more than any other came to summarise Cook's approach, despite being misquoted: that of an 'ethical foreign policy'. Cook and the FCO mission statement had more modestly called for an 'ethical dimension' to foreign policy, but the sexier label stuck in the minds of the media, the public and the opposition parties. There is little doubt that this was due to the higher profile given to such matters by Cook and the Labour Party, as New Labour had hardly invented the theme in British foreign policy, despite the ease with which they had painted the Conservatives (with much help from the latter) as fixated on the amoral pursuit of the national interest. But human rights had over the previous three decades slowly been emerging as an issue in UK foreign policy, with the previous Conservative government establishing a Human Rights Department in the FCO.[7]

What singled out New Labour's approach was its direct attempt to secure the agenda as its own, and the apparent aim of confronting those dictators among Western allies who had always offended the party's conscience (Tory human rights concerns tended to focus on communist oppression). Yet Cook, like so many previous Foreign Secretaries who took on this policy area, soon faced the issue of Britain's large commercial interests and government-approved arms exports to states whose human rights records were far from exemplary. It was therefore easy for many to pick on what seemed apparent contradictions and hypocrisy when it came to the substance of an ethical foreign policy. A more nuanced approach would argue that Cook and New Labour were intent on shoring up the ethical side in the inevitable debate over what Britain could afford to accommodate in terms of financial or economic interests which might be affected by the imposition of sanctions or embargos. Either way, it turned out to be a rocky row for Cook to hoe, not helped by the Prime Minister distancing himself from such concerns and his increasingly clear identification with the business perspective.

This challenge of being prepared to meet new expectations was also evident in the one foreign policy area which New Labour had talked about in some detail while in opposition: Europe. The record of the Major years in this area had been dismal – indeed the Conservative Party had torn itself apart due in large part to divisions over Europe, and officials had despaired of having effective political leadership in their negotiations in Brussels. New Labour and Blair promised a fresh start for UK–EU relations, with Blair echoing John Major's call for Britain to be 'at the heart of Europe'. As Cook later noted, New Labour sought to establish the UK as a player in Europe with a weight equal to that of Germany and France.[8] Compared to the embattled Major, Blair's command of a large Commons majority and a unified party looked likely to allow him to do so. That New Labour appeared much more at ease with Europe was symbolised by Blair addressing the French National Assembly in French, and by Cook being elected the President of the Party of European Socialists in 2001. The new government also immediately took a positive attitude to what was to become the treaty of Amsterdam, accepting the Social Chapter, which the Conservatives had found anathema. Yet, again, it can be debated to what extent this was a genuine transformation of the substance of British policy rather than a change of style, aided by enthusiasm from the rest of the EU for a British government with whom they could do business. One commentator described New Labour as being more of an anti-anti-

Europe party than pro-Europe.[9] In time it became clear that the UK would remain committed to the veto in large areas of policy, maintain suspicions over any communitarisation of foreign and defence policy, and maintain the UK's opt-out on the Schengen agreement. And on the euro the UK and New Labour remained ambivalent, with the increasingly pro-euro Cook being sidelined by an uneasy Blair and an evidently sceptical Brown – who clearly held the reins on this issue.[10]

This does not mean that New Labour or Cook soon came to jettison their hopes for a more positive role in Europe; new means were found to express the UK's desire for a close working relationship. The most significant came at a relatively early stage. The signing of the St Malo agreement in December 1998, by Blair and French President Jacques Chirac, committed Europe's two key military powers to further defence co-operation with a view to creating a viable European Security and Defence Policy (ESDP) – subsequently launched in 1999 at Helsinki. Concerns that this would undermine NATO and the alliance with the United States were dismissed, for once, in London. The experience of Bosnia had highlighted the need for Europe to get its act together on defence. Questions persist, however, as to whether the UK and France shared the same strategic vision at St Malo. More profoundly, some have argued that St Malo was a cheap commitment for New Labour to make, given its difficulties over the euro and the ESDP's de facto dependence on NATO assets.[11] Moreover, on defence as in foreign and security policy, the UK cannot be ignored; it is London's ace in European integration, albeit one that previous governments have not been able easily to play.

The key tension for New Labour, as with all previous British governments bar that of Edward Heath, turned out to be the challenge of balancing the European and US dimensions of Britain's international outlook. Yet to Cook, Blair and large parts of New Labour, looking both ways across the Atlantic and the Channel did not present a dilemma in principle. As Cook himself noted, 'the paradox that anti-Europeans fail to acknowledge is that far from undermining our Special

Relationship with the USA, our membership of the EU is increasingly important to the success of that relationship'.[12] Such attitudes, along with the whole baggage of new approaches to foreign policy, were put to their most powerful test by the war in Kosovo. Labour had watched from the opposition benches as the former Yugoslavia had fallen apart in bloody conflicts aided in part by Europe's inability to act, Washington's indifference and Russia's post-Cold War ambivalence. Preventing a recurrence in Kosovo was something New Labour and Cook were determined to achieve. NATO's Operation Allied Force was presented as a just war, justified by the need to prevent further conflict. New Labour displayed its slick, professional approach to the media in winning the political and public debates about the war. Although Cook later argued that Britain and the US were the key to the action over Kosovo,[13] tensions between Europe and the US simmered throughout. It was the eventual threat of a ground war, which could only have been conducted by the US, coupled with Russian pressure on Serbia, that brought an end to the conflict. While the degree to which the UK played a part in bringing about an eventual Serbian withdrawal can be debated, the language and ideas employed by the UK appeared to signal a very powerful change. At the height of the conflict, on 25 April 1999, Blair delivered a speech in Chicago entitled 'The doctrine of the international community', to which we will return. Suffice to say that it set out a new philosophy of foreign policy, explicitly justifying inter-vention into the internal affairs of other states, largely on humanitarian grounds. Cook agreed with the action over Kosovo, but had not been consulted over the new philosophy. Increasingly it became evident that there were now two versions of 'ethical foreign policy' alive within the New Labour Cabinet, and Cook was to become increasingly uneasy over Blair's interventionist model. This was to be the source of the final rupture between the two men, over Iraq. But by then Cook had been moved out of King Charles Street.

Beyond Europe it was on issues relating to Africa where Cook faced some of his most challenging dilemmas. The aforementioned St Malo summit also saw agreement between the UK and France to work more closely together in Africa; in March 1999 Cook and Hubert Védrine (then French Foreign Minister) made an unprecedented joint visit to Ghana and Côte d'Ivoire, thus transcending some of the traditional Anglo-French competition in west Africa. Cook was also given credit for helping to solve the tensions that surrounded the trial related to the destruction of Pan Am flight 103 over the Scottish town of Lockerbie in December 1988. Libya was persuaded to hand over two accused suspects for trial in the neutral venue of the Netherlands but under Scottish law. In turn this helped pave the way towards the eventual rapprochement between Libya and the West.

Yet it was events in Sierra Leone that posed the biggest test to Cook and the FCO. The FCO and the British high commissioner in Freetown, Sierra Leone's capital, were accused of acting improperly in allowing Sandline International, a British private military company, to supply arms to the supporters of the deposed President Ahmed Tejan Kabbah, in so doing breaking a UN arms embargo. The Prime Minister was untroubled, arguing that the end (of returning a democratically elected government to power) justified the means (of overriding the UN's legitimate attempts to bring an end to the conflict). But both Parliament and the media took a different view, with the eventual report of the Commons Foreign Affairs Committee being sharply critical of the FCO's permanent under-secretary, and therefore by extension of Cook himself.

Cook's demotion to Leader of the House of Commons following the 2001 general election came as a shock, not least to him. While he had suffered some policy setbacks and personal problems, and lacked the political following of other major figures in the party, he was generally seen to have been a success at managing the foreign policy brief. He had helped to refurbish the image of British diplomacy abroad, gaining the respect and support of most foreign colleagues – with the significant exception of Washington, where his pro-American credentials were not deemed convincing. In the two years which followed, his post as Leader of the House gave him a ringside seat, but no active role in foreign policy-making, given the atrophy of Cabinet government under Blair. It pushed him towards his natural backbench (and 'old Labour') constituency, helped by his status as an outstanding Commons performer. His resignation speech on 17 March 2003, widely acknowledged as one of the finest ever made in the House of Commons, made it clear that he did not seek to bring down the government, for which he had fought so hard, but to stop it making a flawed decision lacking international legitimacy. The speech was a landmark, both for the splits which were emerging in New Labour over the alignment of British foreign policy to that of the neo-conservatives in the US, and in the history of what A. J. P. Taylor called 'the troublemakers', that is, the long line of principled dissenters over the course of modern British foreign policy.[14] Cook died suddenly in 2005, which deprived British and European politics and the Labour Party of an incisive mind and powerful orator.

Jack Straw 2001–6

Jack Straw's appointment as Foreign Secretary came as a surprise even to him. Having served as Home Secretary from 1997 to 2001 he had expected to follow the 2001 general election with a move to the Department for Transport. Widely held to be competent, a safe pair of hands, he had been seen as a tough-talking Home Secretary who could be relied upon to handle many delicate issues such as the arrest in London of the late Chilean dictator General Augusto Pinochet. His earlier political career had seen him emerge as a leading student activist, which made it ironic that he now became the minister responsible for MI5, which had once monitored his activities. His credentials as a member of the Labour Party were as solid as Robin Cook's, but compared to the robust and independent Scot, Straw was generally seen as being more pliable.

It was the events of 11 September 2001 which most profoundly shaped the foreign policy agenda that Straw was to face as Foreign Secretary. Led by the Prime Minister, Britain undertook a role that was militarily, diplomatically and politically substantial. While Jacques Chirac was the first foreign leader to visit the US after the attacks, it was Tony Blair who made his unconditional support the clearest.[15] For his part Straw developed and maintained a close working relationship with his US counterpart, Secretary of State Colin Powell. He was later to replicate this with Powell's successor, Condoleezza Rice, building a relationship which included a joint trip to his constituency of Blackburn in return for a visit to her home town of Birmingham, Alabama. Yet it was Blair and his advisers in Downing Street, notably David Manning and Jonathan Powell, who shaped the commitment to the 'war on terror' and to the ensuing invasion of Afghanistan.

The same influences were decisive in the run-up to the Iraq War of 2003. Given the long involvement of British forces in Iraq, the decision to commit Britain to the war, once the decision had been taken (probably early in 2002) in Washington to prosecute it, should have been no surprise. What did make many close observers uncomfortable, including many in the FCO, was that the Prime Minister appeared to have committed the UK to support such action at an early stage, and thus to have given away any real leverage and freedom of manoeuvre. This further fuelled feelings that Britain's reflex commitment was always to the US instead of to Europe, or even to its own interests. Straw was caught in the middle of this, increasingly uneasy but effectively impotent. He seems never to have taken the side of Cook and Clare Short in their increasing attempts to mobilise Cabinet opposition to the prevailing policy, although until the relevant public records are available, we shall not know.

The logic by which Britain advocated war in Iraq was significantly different to that presented by the US, with Blair and Straw placing an emphasis upon international law. For Blair the decision to follow the Bush administration in attacking Iraq was as much a result of his own personal convictions that the action was morally necessary as it was his concern to ensure that Britain always sided with the US and to shape American policy from within rather than by criticism from without.[16] Yet he and Straw realised that the policy could be sold at home and in the wider international community only if it had been legitimised by a UN Security Council resolution. This is why they were so pleased with Resolution 1441 of 8 November 2002, which Colin Powell and the US State Department had worked hard to deliver against the scepticism of the Washington hawks.[17] The resolution – the result of protracted discussions and compromises – offered Iraq a final opportunity to comply with its disarmament obligations, threatening 'serious consequences' if it failed to do so.

Problems soon emerged, however, over the need for a second resolution to authorise the use of force. The compromises of 1441 left plenty of room for interpretation; on the one side the US Vice-President, Dick Cheney, and Secretary of Defense, Donald Rumsfeld, were arguing for immediate action, while on the other France and Germany sought more time for the UN's weapons inspectors. Britain was caught in the middle, with New Labour facing the largest backbench rebellion it had ever suffered together with widespread public unease, culminating in the massive public demonstration of 15 February 2003. For Straw in particular this was a painful dilemma, determined as he was to see both parliamentary approval and a second resolution. Such was his difficulty that he is reported to have sought at the eleventh hour an alternative path, with the UK engaging in post-war operations but not the actual war. However, when pressed by Blair he agreed that 1441 gave all the necessary authorisation required and thus supported what was by then an inevitable war.[18]

The post-war situation has been uncomfortable for Straw – and the US and UK in general – due to both the failure to locate weapons of mass destruction (WMD) and the catalogue of mistakes that has characterised post-war policy. The failure to locate WMD has plagued Blair more than it has the Bush administration, which had framed the

Iraq war in much wider terms. The inquiries of first Lord Hutton and then Lord Butler cleared the Prime Minster and Foreign Secretary of actual misdemeanours, but in the court of public opinion they reinforced the image of how under New Labour the centre of government had become an informal place in which intelligence, policy-making and public relations were blurring into each other, with expert analysis being subject to strong, and often inappropriate, political influence.[19]

The failure to locate WMD also contributed to a general unease at what the UK was gaining from the Iraq policy, and from the policy of remaining close to Washington – what Peter Riddell termed the 'hug them close' approach. In the run-up to the war Blair had sought three assurances from President Bush: first, on the effective reconstruction of Iraq; second, on the central involvement of the UN; and third, on making the resolution of the Israel–Palestine problem the next priority.[20] In the event, these assurances were not, and perhaps could not be, fulfilled: Iraq has fallen into enduring chaos, rather than freedom; the UN has been driven out; and while Bush did commit the US to the creation of a viable Palestinian state, the resolution of the conflict between Israel and the Palestinians seems today (after the 2006 war in Lebanon) more distant than ever. Indeed, as early as April 2004, Bush's approval of the unilateral Israeli policy of withdrawal from Gaza and then the building of the 'security wall' effectively discarded the Middle East peace 'road map' to which Blair thought Bush had given his commitment. It was this change that provoked fifty-two retired prominent British diplomats to write an open letter to the Prime Minister, stating their deep misgivings over the approach he was taking in the Middle East. The letter, widely seen as reflecting the silent opinions of the serving diplomatic community – and thus placing Straw in an invidious position – criticised the approach taken to Iraq and the fact that 'the conduct of the war in Iraq has made it clear that there was no effective plan for the post-Saddam settlement'.[21] It pressed the Prime Minister to be prepared, when necessary, to disagree with Washington.

Relations were by now just as uneasy with the continental governments which New Labour had attempted to cultivate over the previous
five years. British relations with France and Germany in particular
became stormy, with a renewal of the Franco-German axis which the
UK had tried for so long to break apart. A meeting to discuss European
defence in Brussels in April 2003 between France, Germany, Belgium
and Luxembourg (the so-called 'chocolate summit'), appeared to up the
ante in terms of the competition between the EU and NATO. Yet it was
clear that progress would be slow without Britain, and the move
brought forth a conciliatory response from London, on which both
Blair and Straw seem to have been agreed.

Indeed Britain, France and Germany were still working together in
developing a trilateral relationship over some foreign and defence policy
issues. While Blair and Chirac had clashed bitterly on Iraq, their
officials nevertheless continued to discuss the creation of a common
European armaments agency and co-operation on proposed new
aircraft carriers. The EU's draft 'Security Strategy', first circulated in
June 2003, also reflected some joint working between the big three,
without whose agreement it could never have seen the light of day, let
alone have been agreed as quickly as it was, in the Brussels Council of
December 2003.[22] France and Britain naturally shared a more active
and more global approach to foreign policy than most EU member
states, and they were keen to draw Germany into taking on more
responsibilities, even if full membership of the UN Security Council
was proving difficult for Berlin to achieve. Most notably, the 'big three'
took the initiative to head off a dangerous crisis with Iran. Straw was the
first Foreign Secretary to visit Tehran since the Iranian Revolution of
1979, also stating on a number of occasions that an attack on Iran was
'inconceivable', something which may have put him at odds with
Washington and the Prime Minister and eventually contributed to his
demise.

Set against a backdrop of European enlargement, the ideas of long-
term foreign and security policy co-operation also fed into the agenda

focused on the European constitution, proposing as it did, inter alia, the creation of a common armaments agency, a European Foreign Minister (to be assisted by a European External Action Service) and a President of Europe, replacing the cumbersome rotating presidency. The draft constitution was seen by some integrationists as a victory for the UK, reinforcing in particular British ideas on the 'flexible' economy; in Britain, however, it was viewed with unease, especially the provisions detailing closer co-operation in foreign affairs and the very name 'constitution'. With a general election approaching New Labour risked losing votes to a Conservative opposition campaigning against the constitution. Straw is widely credited with having convinced Blair to agree to a referendum sometime after the election, thus avoiding the risk of the constitution becoming an electoral liability. Also, by pushing Britain's final decision to the end of the ratification queue, the chance was provided that another member state would reject the constitution first. And so it proved. Events in France and the Netherlands spared New Labour from having to engage in a serious debate about the UK's role in Europe, a debate which successive governments, all too aware of the potential for party splits, have done everything to avoid.

Straw oversaw one important change which has received little attention, namely the internal reform of the Foreign and Commonwealth Office. The reforms, begun under Robin Cook, have attempted both to reconnect the FCO with a fast-changing domestic society, for instance through more effective recruitment among ethnic minorities, and to ensure that its management structures were capable of responding to the wide spectrum of new challenges, from the EU's growing importance in home affairs to digital diplomacy and the provision of assistance to British nationals caught up in natural or man-made disasters. Adapting to these needs has been organised through a range of reviews such as 'Foresight', a consultative exercise which sought to define a vision for the FCO.[23] They eventually led to the FCO's Strategy Document, setting out the UK's key priorities in foreign policy and explaining how the FCO would efficiently organise itself to realise them. Such restructuring has not been without its complaints, either from within the FCO or from without; external consultants Collinson Grant in particular were reported to have been very critical of the FCO's management.[24] Seen in part as a legacy of New Labour's desire to see the foreign policy process opened up, the reforms are also a powerful demonstration of the FCO coming to terms with UK foreign policy-making no longer being the preserve of the FCO but something shared with the rest of Whitehall and in particular with 10 Downing Street.

Straw's move in 2006 to the lower-key position of Leader of the House of Commons – a path taken by Cook – was seen as a demotion, just as Cook's had been, and highlighted the Prime Minister's power, even high-handedness, over the FCO. Rumours abounded that the move was due to pressure from a Washington unhappy with Straw's stated position on Iran, a position the Prime Minister found it increasingly difficult to support, on the grounds that ruling out the use of force ab initio unnecessarily boxed in Western diplomacy. The situation was not helped by the view that Straw's line was as much about securing his position among Labour supporters hostile to the war as it was about the merits of the issue, and that he was manoeuvring to become close to Gordon Brown, due – it seemed – to inherit Blair's crown. Straw was replaced by Margaret Beckett, the first female Foreign Secretary, and a senior member of the government (albeit one with little experience of foreign policy), who immediately found herself plunged into, first, intense UN Security Council negotiations on Iran, and then the crisis of summer 2006 in Lebanon. The departure of yet another established and confident Foreign Secretary could only lend weight to the increasing role in foreign affairs played by the Prime Minister, a role to which we now turn.

Tony Blair

No discussion of the Foreign Secretaries or foreign policy of New Labour would be complete without a separate discussion of Tony Blair, who has asserted himself over all three of his Foreign Secretaries, even if he did not go so far as the former Italian Prime Minister Silvio Berlusconi, who did the job of Foreign Minister himself for eleven months of his premiership. During Blair's period as opposition leader, aside from the issue of Europe, he showed little inclination to comment on foreign affairs, to the extent that Peter Mandelson was once driven to wonder 'won't TB fight wars?' on a draft Labour Party document that made no reference to defence.[25] Once settled in office, like all other Prime Ministers Blair was drawn into foreign affairs. Indeed, he came to revel in them, and the place in history which seems to concern him so much is likely to be defined by his international record.

This has been a product of several factors which deserve brief mention. First, there is the powerful role played by Gordon Brown in domestic policy, which has inevitably meant that the PM would engage more closely with foreign affairs. Brown seems to have deliberately remained remote from foreign policy questions, which had implications for Cabinet decision-making on Iraq. Second, international affairs since 1997 – and especially events following 11 September – have driven the Prime Minister to take a more proactive role than might otherwise have been the case. International relations consist of a series of crises, but the challenges of first the Balkans and then 9/11 would have been major priorities for any British government. Third, the Prime Minister's strong personal beliefs have shaped a distinctive approach – which we may loosely term 'humanitarian interventionism' – to international politics. Fourth, these personal opinions chimed with the strong internationalist orientation of the Labour Party (even if in the end they were to clash with the competing pacifist tradition). Finally, the PM's informal approach to policy-making has permitted his personality and the views of his close advisers to have an unusually powerful impact on key decisions.[26]

In recent decades, with the spread of external relations across most areas of government, the role of the Prime Minister's office has become increasingly central to the idea of 'joined-up' foreign policy. As Lord Owen powerfully argues in this book, this has been lacking in several key policy areas due to Blair's reliance upon informal and structurally limited advice; something which Anthony Seldon touches on with his idea of a '*den*ocracy' at the heart of the Blair approach to governing, a reference to the regular informal gatherings of close advisers in the PM's office, known to insiders as 'the den'.[27] In academic terms this has helped to show that while Prime Minister Blair has downgraded Cabinet government he has not achieved 'presidential' power. Thus, in the terms of the political scientist Richard Heffernan, the position of Prime Minister is more akin to one of 'prime ministerial pre-dominance': the Prime Minister leads, but cannot always command, the 'core executive'; he directs, but does not fully control, its policy development; and he manages, but cannot wholly dominate, the legislature.[28] As Lord Owen demonstrated, when Blair has tried to go beyond this in foreign policy he has faced serious difficulties.

Blair's very personal approach to foreign affairs might be termed a 'Blair doctrine'.[29] While it is the case that before entering Downing Street Blair said little about foreign policy as such, the whole agenda of New Labour revolved around the concepts of globalisation, inter-dependence and the network economy. A particular emphasis was placed upon the end of sovereignty as understood in the Cold War (or even the 'Westphalian') era, with an emphasis instead being upon co-operation with European or other international partners, and a relaxed attitude (in principle) to issues of independence. This can be located in a wider debate in international relations about the concepts of sovereignty, rights and justice; indeed Blair's approach was epitomised in his aforementioned 'doctrine of the international community', which argued that intervention in the internal affairs of other countries is justified on humanitarian grounds. These grounds were widened after 11 September 2001 to include security – the hosting of terrorists and the possession of WMD. In Blair's Labour conference speech following the attacks of September 11, he felt the compulsion of change: 'This is a moment to seize. The kaleidoscope has been shaken. The pieces are in flux. Soon they will settle again. Before they do, let us reorder the world around us.' The interventions in Kosovo, Sierra Leone and East Timor had largely been on human rights grounds; in Afghanistan and then Iraq security was to be at the fore. Deeply embedded in the outlook was a role for Britain as the 'bridge' between the US and Europe; essential if the Atlantic alliance was to remain the fundamental axis for the preservation and advancement of a liberal world order.[30]

To some extent Blair's previous willingness to see sovereignty as out-moded, and to envisage limits on Britain's own sovereignty, was undermined by his increasingly nationalist discourse about the importance of Britain's special role, and by his unwillingness to pay more than lip service to European integration. There is one area, however, where the Prime Minister certainly did not insist on a strict interpretation of British sovereign rights – that is, in relations with the US. Both Blair and George W. Bush strongly supported the necessity of pre-emptive strikes against failing or rogue states in the aftermath of 9/11. However, the relationship was deeply asymmetrical. While the President always insisted that no one else would take decisions for the US, the Prime Minister fell in behind the US when he proved unable to persuade Washington of his own preferred course of action. Worse, he seems to have committed himself to supporting a war in Iraq at a very early stage, before proper discussions had taken place in Cabinet, let alone the House of Commons. Many also hold the view that a blind eye was turned to the US's use of UK airports first for 'rendition' flights and then for the transporting of munitions to Israel during the 2006 war in Lebanon, despite the evident hostility in Britain to the use of camps such as that at Guantánamo Bay, and to the idea of taking sides in the Israel–Hezbollah conflict.

Fundamental differences, however, did exist between Blair and Bush. While both advocated the spread of liberal democracy, for Bush this entailed the right of the US to take pre-emptive action to assert American power, and without the constraints of multilateralism. Such an exceptionally ambitious approach was rooted in neo-conservative thinking.[31] Blair, on the other hand, wished to be prominent in all multilateral fora, which meant seeking legitimacy for interventions through the UN and accepting that few problems could have unilateral solutions – this, indeed, was the logic of the globalisation discourse.

If Blair and Bush had indeed embraced the same agenda, then choosing to be close to the US would have offered Blair a chance to realise such ideals as removing dictators, upholding human rights, confronting states with WMD, bringing international terrorists to justice and bringing peace to the Middle East. But as we have heard, and in line with the experience of previous Prime Ministers, the Americans seemed to notice Blair only 'when his suit matched what they wanted to wear anyway'.[32] The doctrines were incompatible, based as they were on opposite experiences of power: the US as the global hegemon, Britain as a post-imperial power with a willingness to wage war, but bound by commitments to institutions and treaties which British opinion was uneasy about breaking. Blair has unsuccessfully tried to bridge this divide, with damaging consequences for the public diplomacy and other forms of 'soft power' on which Britain increasingly relies.

New Labour's foreign policy legacy

With Tony Blair in the final period of his premiership we need to begin defining the foreign policy legacy which he, and his Foreign Secretaries, will leave behind them. Has New Labour changed British foreign policy radically compared to its Conservative predecessors?

There has, of course, been no wiping clean of the slate. The complexities of international relations do not permit it, especially for countries such as Britain, with their extensive historical baggage. The Anglo-American relationship has been central to all British Prime Ministers since 1940. Even Edward Heath, who chose to turn towards Europe, was defined by it through the crises of 1973–4. Yet New Labour has gone against what seemed to be the emerging trend of a weakening Special Relationship, reaffirming its importance with a vengeance. This was understandable during the presidency of Bill Clinton: Labour had learnt much from his informal style of politics, while relations with the Democrats in opposition had been good. What was surprising was the determination to stick close to the neo-conservative Bush presidency, albeit advised by Clinton himself. There were many issues on which not only did British and American opinion diverge, but their objective interests seemed at odds. Nonetheless, the British government under Blair has been willing to adopt a different public position from that of Washington only when little has been at stake. No doubt this was in part determined by the trauma of 9/11, after which Blair accepted the 'for us or against us' logic of George W. Bush's stance. But as time went on, especially over Iraq, it meant that he was increasingly in conflict with his own party, and with the FCO. Robin Cook had been moved on for the potential threat he posed as an alternative pole of foreign policy-making. Jack Straw left the FCO not because of his open rebellion, but because of myriad signs that he had come to share the views of his officials more than those of 10 Downing Street. Blair would allow no crack to open up in the Atlantic bridge which he had made his priority.

This meant, by extension, that although New Labour genuinely wanted positive relations with its EU partners, if a choice had to be made then Europe would be sacrificed. Indeed, as over Iraq, Britain was not above playing the divide-and-rule game (in this case using the candidate members from eastern Europe) to prevent a major challenge being mounted to the preferred policy line. The row of 2002–3 over Iraq showed that Blair's government would readily sacrifice its self-proclaimed bridge-building function between Washington and the EU if the substance of Anglo-American strategy seemed endangered. In contrast to the empty-chair days of the end of the Major government, and to the relentless negativity of the Thatcher years, New Labour has certainly made Britain into a more powerful player in the EU – as demonstrated by its ability to create the ESDP and Lisbon agendas, and to drive forward the enlargement to twenty-seven member states – but this has been at the cost of setting clear limits to the future evolution of EU policies and institutions, epitomised by the UK's absence from the euro and thus from macroeconomic policy-making.

How is history likely to treat the records of the two men who were foreign secretaries in the years 1997–2006, that is, Cook and Straw? Cook's time in office saw Labour taking responsibility for the British state, at home and abroad, for the first time since 1979. The party was desperate to show that it had shed the image of flakiness on foreign policy which the Conservatives had found it easy to pin on their opponents. Inexperience in government had been a major factor weighing against New Labour. Yet Cook did not make the mistake of overcompensating. Indeed he was determined to bring a new tone and distinctive values to bear on foreign policy, with his stress on human rights and on greater openness in the policy process. By no means a pacifist, he was willing to support the war over Kosovo, even if he had increasing misgivings over the close alignment of British and American policies. On Europe, he showed himself capable of learning from experience, and succeeded in protecting British interests by taking a generally constructive line – and by his high professional competence. Given that his post-FCO judgements on the Iraq War have largely been vindicated, it seems likely that posterity will see him as one of the ablest occupants of the FCO since 1945.

Straw's term was shaped by events starting with 11 September. Like Cook, he has been uneasy at taking military action in contravention of international law, preferring multilateral solutions. Ultimately, however – like the rest of the Cabinet, apart from Cook – he chose to stand by the Prime Minister's policies. He was thus forced to accept the subordination of the FCO to No. 10, which is understandable to the extent that his only leverage came from the 'nuclear option' of the threat of resignation. Straw was more of a trimmer than Cook, only distancing himself from Blair once it became clear that events were turning out badly. His major success was over the draft European Constitution, where his preference for a referendum turned out to have been a tactical triumph. His removal from the FCO, coming as soon as it did after the triumphal welcoming of Condoleezza Rice to his Blackburn constituency, demonstrated at a stroke his own weakness and Blair's willingness to cut down any poppy which grew too tall.

Both Cook and Straw shared the strains of the ever greater demands on the Foreign Secretary's role, something which had been evident at least since the days of David Owen in the 1970s. The increasing amount of travel, the demands of the 24-hour news cycle, the information overload, and the growing involvement of other government agencies in both foreign and European policy have all belied the notion that diplomacy is becoming redundant. Cook and Straw also had to cope with the increasing assertiveness of the Prime Minister in foreign policy, admittedly an intermittent problem since the days of Palmerston. As argued above, Blair has imposed both a powerful individual style of decision-making, and an increasingly controversial line of policy.

One element common to the thinking of Cook, Straw and Blair has been their assumption that Britain must be a major international player, legitimised as much through the notion of 'a force for good' as through the traditional assertion of 'the national interest'. Blair's preference for a peripatetic style of world statesmanship has reinforced this approach and indeed the image of Britain as an important state. Like Margaret Thatcher and Mikhail Gorbachev, Blair has a much higher reputation abroad than at home, while most foreign observers associate British policy more with him than with any of his three Foreign Secretaries. Yet this observation must be qualified: in many parts of the world, especially those alienated by Western policy, he is seen as 'Bush's poodle', while the war in Iraq will prove a bitter legacy, damaging his overall reputation.

It is clear that under New Labour the UK has pursued an assertive foreign policy, with increasing global reach, much in contrast with the defensiveness of the Labour years under Wilson and Callaghan. The confidence, and even the sense of moral rectitude, on display have produced a sharp debate on both the nature of the 'ethics' being pursued and the issue of overstretch. Britain is only an upper-middle power and struggles to live up to the range of commitments it has taken on during the Blair years. Many of the professionals in the FCO and Ministry of Defence, who have gradually influenced most of the ministers appointed to be their political masters, have grave doubts about both the general direction of policy and some of its particulars, notably in the Middle East. These debates and tensions will not go away, whoever occupies Downing Street in the future. Britain as a country is ambivalent about the extent of its responsibilities in international affairs, while its multicultural society has opened up new cracks in the domestic base. Foreign policy, and the roles of its key practitioners, seem certain to remain at the centre of our notions of who we are and what we should be doing.

Biographies of the contributors

William Wallace

William Wallace (Lord Wallace of Saltaire) is Emeritus Professor of International Relations at the London School of Economics and Political Science, the Liberal Democrats' spokesman on foreign affairs in the British House of Lords and deputy leader of the Liberal Democrat group in the Lords. He was a member of the House of Lords European Union Committee from 1996 to 2001, and chair of its Justice and Home Affairs Sub-Committee from 1997 to 2000.

Professor Wallace took his PhD in government at Cornell University in 1968. He was director of studies at the Royal Institute of International Affairs (Chatham House) between 1978 and 1990. From 1990 to 1995 he was the Walter F. Hallstein Fellow at St Antony's College, Oxford; between 1993 and 1996 he was concurrently Professor of International Relations at the Central European University in Budapest. He was appointed Reader in International Relations at the LSE in 1995 and Professor of International Relations in 1998. Professor Wallace was awarded an honorary degree by the Free University of Brussels in 1992. The French government awarded him the Ordre Nationale du Mérite in 1995 and the Légion d'Honneur in 2005.

He has written extensively on European international politics and transatlantic relations. He is also an occasional columnist for the *Financial Times.* Recent publications include *Rethinking European Order: West European Responses 1989–97* (with Robin Niblett and others; Basingstoke: Palgrave, 2001); *Non-State Actors in World Politics* (with Daphne Josselin and others; Basingstoke: Palgrave, 2001); *Looking after the Neighbours: Europe's New Neighbourhood Policy* (Paris: Notre Europe, 2004); and *Policy-Making in the European Union* (with Helen Wallace and others; Oxford: Oxford University Press, 5th edition 2005).

The Rt Hon. the Lord Owen CH

David Owen was born in 1938. He was a member of Parliament for Plymouth Sutton from 1966 to 1974, and for Plymouth Devonport from 1974 to 1992, during which time, under Labour governments, he was Navy Minister, Health Minister and Foreign Secretary. He was a founder of the Social Democratic Party in 1981 and its leader from 1983 to 1990. From 1992 to 1995 Lord Owen was the EU peace negotiator in the former Yugoslavia. He was created a life peer in 1992.

His current business interests include the chair of Yukos International BV and Global Natural Energy, the deputy chair of Europe Steel and a non-executive directorship of the US pharmaceutical company Abbott Laboratories. He is also chairman of New Europe, chancellor of Liverpool University, director of the Centre for International Health and Cooperation and president of the Enabling Partnership.

Lord Owen has served on a number of independent commissions, including the Independent Commission on Disarmament and Security Issues, the Independent Commission on International Humanitarian Issues and the Carnegie Commission on Preventing Armed Conflict. He was chairman of Humanitas from 1990 to 2001, a charitable organisation dedicated to public education on humanitarian issues.

Lord Owen has written a number of books, including *Human Rights* (London: Jonathan Cape, 1978); *Face the Future* (London: Jonathan Cape, 1981); his autobiography, *Time to Declare* (London: Michael Joseph, 1991); and *Balkan Odyssey* (London: Victor Gollancz, 1995). He has also compiled an anthology of poetry, *Seven Ages* (London: Michael Joseph, 1992).

The Rt Hon. the Lord Carrington KG GCMG CH MC

Lord Carrington is a former Secretary General of NATO, a former Secretary of State for Foreign and Commonwealth Affairs and Minister of Overseas Development, and a former Secretary of State for Defence. He has also been Chairman of the Conservative Party, First Lord of the Admiralty and British high commissioner to Australia.

Peter Alexander Rupert Carington (the family name has only one R), the only son of the fifth Lord Carrington, was born in 1919 and educated at Eton and the Royal Military College, Sandhurst. He succeeded to the title on his father's death in 1938. He was commissioned into the Grenadier Guards and served throughout the Second World War, taking part in the campaign in north-western Europe, reaching the rank of major and being awarded the Military Cross. He resigned his commission in 1945 and took up farming.

Lord Carrington began to take an active part in the work of Parliament in 1946. He was an opposition whip in the House of Lords during the two post-war Labour governments and, when the Conservatives returned to power in 1951, he became a parliamentary secretary at the Ministry of Agriculture and Fisheries at the age of thirty-two – one of the youngest members of government.

In 1956 he was appointed United Kingdom high commissioner to Australia. (He has family links with that country going back to the 1880s and his father was born there.) In 1959 he relinquished his appointment in Australia and returned to the United Kingdom, where he again took up political work.

He was appointed First Lord of the Admiralty and a Privy Counsellor in 1959, and in 1963 became leader of the House of Lords. From 1964 until 1970, and also from 1974 to 1979, he was a member of the shadow Cabinet and leader of the opposition in the Lords. In the 1970 Conservative government he was appointed Secretary of State for Defence, relinquishing this office on becoming Secretary of State for Energy, a position he held until the general election of February 1974.

Between 1972 and June 1974 he was also chairman of the Conservative Party.

Lord Carrington was appointed Secretary of State for Foreign and Commonwealth Affairs following the return of the Conservatives to office after the election in May 1979. He was chairman of the Lancaster House Conference at the end of 1979, which led to the solution of the Rhodesian problem and the formation of the independent republic of Zimbabwe. He resigned as Secretary of State in April 1982. In 1984 he was appointed Secretary-General of NATO, a position he held until 1988.

Lord Carrington received the Military Cross in 1945 and in 1958 was appointed Knight Commander of the Order of St Michael and St George for his services in Australia. In 1983 he was appointed a Companion of Honour, and two years later was installed as a Knight of the Garter. In 1988 he was appointed Knight Grand Cross of the Order of St Michael and St George. After the House of Lords Act 1999 removed the automatic right of hereditary peers to sit in the House of Lords, he was created a life peer as Lord Carington of Upton.

Away from politics, Lord Carrington is chancellor of Reading University and has been a director of various banking and business concerns.

Lord Carrington is married and has a son, the Hon. Rupert Carington, and two daughters, Alexandra, the Hon. Mrs de Bunsen, and the Hon. Virginia Carington. Iona, Lady Carrington is the younger daughter of the late Sir Francis McClean AFC, one of the pioneers of flying in the United Kingdom.

The Rt Hon. the Lord Howe of Aberavon CH QC

Geoffrey Howe served as a Cabinet minister for all but the last three weeks of Margaret Thatcher's government: as Chancellor of the Exchequer (1979–83), as Foreign Secretary (1983–89) and finally as Deputy Prime Minister (1989–90).

Born in Port Talbot in 1926, Lord Howe was educated at Winchester and Trinity Hall, Cambridge. Called to the Bar in 1952 and appointed Queen's Counsel in 1965, he served in Edward Heath's government as Solicitor General (1970–2) and Minister for Trade and Consumer Affairs (1972–4). He was responsible for the preparation and passage through Parliament of the principal legislation providing for Britain's membership of the EEC and for the 1986 enlargement and 1992 single market programme.

Lord Howe served as chairman of the International Monetary Fund Interim Committee (1982–3) and attended eleven World Economic Summits (1979–89). International advisory boards on which he has served include those of J. P. Morgan, Stanford University, the Carlyle Partnership and Fuji (Mitzuho) Bank. He served as chairman of the Framlington Russian Investment Fund (1994–2003) and on the Advisory Council of the Ukrainian Parliament (1991–8).

As Foreign Secretary, Lord Howe was responsible for the negotiation with the People's Republic of China of the 1984 Joint Declaration on the future of Hong Kong and is now president of the Great Britain–China Centre.

Geoffrey Howe was knighted in 1970. He entered the House of Lords in 1992 and was created a Companion of Honour in 1996.

Lord Howe is married to Elspeth, Lady Howe of Idlicote. They have two daughters, Caroline, the Hon. Mrs Ralph and Amanda, the Hon. Mrs Glanvill, and a son, the Hon. Alexander Howe.

The Rt Hon. the Lord Hurd of Westwell CH CBE PC

Lord Hurd retired as Foreign Secretary in July 1995, after a distinguished career in government spanning sixteen years.

After positions as Minister of State in the Foreign Office and the Home Office, he served as Secretary of State for Northern Ireland from 1984 to 1985, Home Secretary from 1985 to 1989 and Foreign Secretary from 1989 to 1995 in the governments of Margaret Thatcher and John Major.

Douglas Hurd was born in 1930. Educated at Eton and Trinity College, Cambridge, he obtained a first class degree in history and was president of the Cambridge Union in 1952. After joining the diplomatic service, he went on to serve the Foreign Office in Peking, New York (for the UN) and Rome. He ran Edward Heath's private office from 1968 to 1970 and acted as his political secretary at 10 Downing Street from 1970 to 1974. He was MP for Oxfordshire Mid (later Witney) from 1974 to 1993, and for Witney from 1993 to 1997. He was appointed a Privy Counsellor in 1982 and a Companion of Honour in 1996, and was created a life peer in 1997.

Lord Hurd was appointed deputy chairman of NatWest Markets and a main board director of NatWest Group in 1995, retiring from the board in April 1999 and leaving the NatWest Group at the end of January 2000. In early 1998 he became deputy chairman of Coutts & Co. He was chairman of the Advisory Committee of Hawkpoint Partners Ltd from 1998 until 2001, and is now a senior adviser to the company. He is chairman of the German–British Forum and of CEDR (Centre for Dispute Resolution).

Lord Hurd was chairman of the Prison Reform Trust from 1998 until January 2001, becoming honorary president in October 2001. He was chairman of British Invisibles from 1997 until April 2000. He became a member of the Royal Commission on the Reform of the House of Lords in February 1999, and a member of the Appointments Commission in the summer of 2000. In September 1999 he was appointed as the High Steward of Westminster Abbey. He was appointed president of the Royal Institute of International Affairs in September 2001.

Lord Hurd lives in Oxfordshire with his wife Judy and their son, the Hon. Philip Hurd, and daughter, the Hon. Jessica Hurd. He has three grown-up sons from his first marriage.

His other pursuits include writing, walking and reading. He was chairman of the 1998 Booker Prize for Fiction. His recent publications include *The Search for Peace* (London: Little, Brown, 1997), *The Shape of Ice* (a novel; London: Little, Brown, 1998), *Ten Minutes to Turn the Devil* (short stories; London: Little, Brown, 1999), *Image in the Water* (a novel; London: Little, Brown, 2001) and *Memoirs* (London: Little, Brown, 2003).

Sir Malcolm Rifkind KCMG QC MP

Malcolm Rifkind was born in Edinburgh in 1946. He was educated at George Watson's College and Edinburgh University, where he studied law before taking a postgraduate degree in political science. While at university he took part in an overland expedition to the Middle East and India. He also appeared on *University Challenge*.

Between 1967 and 1969 he lived in Rhodesia (now Zimbabwe) and taught at the local university. He travelled widely around southern Africa and wrote his postgraduate thesis on the politics of land in Rhodesia. While in Africa he met his wife, Edith, whose parents had emigrated there when she was a small child.

On return to Britain he was called to the Bar and practised as an advocate until 1979. He was appointed a Queen's Counsel in 1985.

In 1970 he fought his first parliamentary campaign and from 1970 to 1974 he was a local councillor in Edinburgh. In 1974 he was elected as Conservative MP for Edinburgh Pentlands and represented that constituency until 1997.

Sir Malcolm was appointed to the front bench in 1975 but resigned over devolution in 1977. In 1979, when the Conservatives were returned to power under Margaret Thatcher, he was appointed parliamentary under-secretary of state, first at the Scottish Office and then, at the time of the Falklands War, at the Foreign and Commonwealth Office, being promoted to Minister of State in 1983.

He became a member of the Cabinet in 1986 as Secretary of State for Scotland. In 1990 he became Minister of Transport and in 1992 Secretary of State for Defence. From 1995 to 1997 he was Foreign Secretary. He was one of only four ministers to serve throughout the whole Prime Ministership of both Margaret Thatcher and John Major. In 1997 he was appointed Knight Commander of the Order of St Michael and St George in recognition of his public service.

Since 1997 Sir Malcolm has worked in the private sector and has assisted a number of companies as a director or consultant. He is currently non-executive chairman of Alliance Medical Holdings and of ArmorGroup. He has also been active in a number of voluntary organisations.

Between 1997 and 2004 he remained active in the political world on radio and TV and in the press. He was invited by William Hague to attend a number of shadow Cabinet meetings and assisted with policy formulation as well as fighting his former parliamentary seat in 2002.

In 2004 Sir Malcolm was adopted as the Conservative parliamentary candidate for Kensington & Chelsea, and was re-elected to Parliament as the member for that constituency in May 2005. He has since been active with local residents and voluntary organisations on a range of issues throughout the constituency. He served as the Shadow Secretary of State for Work & Pensions and Welfare Reform until December 2005.

Sir Malcolm and Lady Rifkind have a daughter, Caroline, and a son, Hugo, both of whom live and work in London.

Christopher Hill

Christopher Hill is Sir Patrick Sheehy Professor of International Relations at the University of Cambridge and director of the university's Centre of International Studies. From 1974 to 2004 he taught in the Department of International Relations at the London School of Economics and Political Science, where he was the Montague Burton Professor.

He has published widely in the areas of foreign policy analysis and general international relations, his most recent books being *The Changing Politics of Foreign Policy* (Basingstoke: Palgrave Macmillan, 2003) and *International Relations and the European Union* (edited with Michael Smith; Oxford: Oxford University Press, 2005). He is also the author of *Cabinet Decisions on Foreign Policy: The British Experience 1938–1941* (Cambridge: Cambridge University Press, 1991). He is a past chair of the British International Studies Association, and was an elected member of the Chatham House Council between 1998 and 2004.

Tim Oliver

Tim Oliver is completing a PhD in the Department of International Relations at the London School of Economics and Political Science. His thesis explores the nature of the contemporary British state and the making of foreign policy. His principal research interests also include British foreign policy, UK–EU and UK–US relations, Whitehall and European foreign and defence policy. He has published widely on British foreign policy including co-authored chapters in the books *Developments in British Politics 8* (ed. Patrick Dunleavy et al.; Basingstoke: Palgrave Macmillan, 2006), *The Europeanization of British Politics* (ed. Ian Bache and Andrew Jordan; Basingstoke: Palgrave Macmillan, 2006) and *The Atlantic Alliance under Stress: US–European Relations after Iraq* (ed. David M. Andrews; Cambridge: Cambridge University Press, 2005). He has worked in the European Parliament and the House of Lords. He also runs the British International Studies Association Working Group on British Foreign Policy.

Notes

Introduction

1. A senior member of the negotiating team told me this when discussing the administrative implications of joining.

Lord Owen's lecture

1. Lord Carrington, *Reflect on Things Past: The Memoirs of Lord Carrington* (London: Collins, 1988), p. 372.
2. Percy Cradock, *In Pursuit of British Interests: Reflections on Foreign Policy under Margaret Thatcher and John Major* (London: John Murray, 1997) p. 9.
3. Geoffrey Howe, *Conflict of Loyalty* (London: Macmillan, 1994), p. 474.
4. Nigel Lawson, *The View from No. 11: Memoirs of a Tory Radical* (London: Bantam Press, 1992).
5. Ibid., p. 893.
6. Ibid.
7. Margaret Thatcher, *The Downing Street Years 1979–90* (London: HarperCollins, 1993), p. 555.
8. *A Memorandum by the Secretary of State for Foreign and Commonwealth Affairs, The Rt Hon. Dr David Owen MP, 26 July 1977.*
9. Christopher Meyer, *DC Confidential: The Controversial Memoirs of Britain's Ambassador to the US at the Time of 9/11 and the Iraq War* (London: Weidenfeld & Nicolson, 2005).

Lord Carrington's lecture

1. Julius Nyerere, the then President of Tanzania.

Lord Howe's lecture

1. Geoffrey Howe, *Conflict of Loyalty* (London: Macmillan, 1994), pp. 309–10.
2. Margaret Thatcher, speech, Winston Churchill Foundation Award dinner, 27 September 1983.
3. Howe, *Conflict of Loyalty*, p. 322.
4. Yuri Andropov was Soviet leader from November 1982 until his death in February 1984. Chernenko succeeded him but he in turn died in March 1985.
5. Pierre Trudeau, Prime Minister of Canada 1968–79 and 1980–4.
6. *World Today*, March 1989, pp. 41–2.
7. Margaret Thatcher, *The Downing Street Years 1979–90* (London: HarperCollins, 1993), p. 415.
8. The then President of Tanzania.
9. Hansard, 14 September 2001.
10. The then US assistant Secretary of Defense.
11. Speech, Royal United Services Institute, 15 March 1985.
12. Thatcher, *Downing Street Years*, p. 469.
13. Ibid., p. 336.
14. Ibid., pp. 710–11.

Lord Hurd's lecture

1. Douglas Hurd, *Memoirs* (London: Little, Brown, 2003), pp. 444–76.
2. US Secretary of State 1977–80.
3. Kofi Annan, 'Intervention', 35th Annual Ditchley Foundation Lecture, 26 June 1998. The Ditchley Foundation was established in 1958 to advance international learning and to bring transatlantic and other experts together to discuss the world's problems. It is based at Ditchley Park in Oxfordshire.
4. Tony Blair, 'Doctrine of the International Community', Economic Club, Chicago, 24 April 1999.
5. Douglas Hurd, *The Search for Peace* (London: Little, Brown, 1997).
6. Lord Alexander of Weedon QC, 'Iraq: Pax Americana and the Rule of Law', Justice Annual Lecture 2003, 14 October 2003.
7. Hurd, *Memoirs*.

Sir Malcolm Rifkind's lecture

1. Incidentally, both this lecture and my subject were decided long before either the LSE or I had realised that the lecture would be given on the day of President Bush's arrival for a state visit to the UK.
2. Douglas Hurd, *Memoirs* (London: Little, Brown, 2003), pp. 467–8.

Afterword

1. John Kampfner, *Blair's Wars* (London: Free Press, 2003). The six wars in which Britain engaged between 1997 and 2006 are: Operation Desert Fox (Iraq, 1998), Kosovo (1999), Sierra Leone (2000), the 'war on terror', Afghanistan (2001) and Iraq (2003). Blair has also committed British troops to East Timor (1999) and the EU-led mission in the Democratic Republic of Congo (2003).

2. It is clearly too early to essay any judgement on Margaret Beckett, who replaced Straw (once more to general surprise) in June 2006.

3. See Rhiannon Vickers, 'Robin Cook', in Kevin Theakston (ed.), *British Foreign Secretaries since 1974* (London: Routledge, 2004).

4. See John Kampfner, *Robin Cook* (London: Victor Gollancz, 1998).

5. See Vickers, 'Robin Cook'.

6. 'Robin Cook's speech on the government's ethical foreign policy', *Guardian*, 12 May 1997.

7. The pursuit of human rights in the Conference on Security and Co-operation in Europe from the early 1970s onwards had been largely a bipartisan affair, while it had been the Conservative government of Margaret Thatcher which had negotiated Zimbabwean independence in 1980 (at the time this seemed like a blow for freedom and democracy).

8. Robin Cook, *The Point of Departure,* (London: Simon and Schuster, 2003), p. 130.

9. Brendan Donnelly, *The Euro and British Politics* (London: Federal Trust, 2005).

10. See Anthony Seldon, *Blair: The Final Verdict,* (London, Free Press, 2004).

11. Robert Dover, 'The Prime Minister and the Core Executive: A Liberal Intergovernmentalist Reading of UK Defence Policy Formulation 1997–2000', *British Journal of Politics and International Relations* (2005), vol. 7, no. 4.

12. Robin Cook, 'Britain's future in Europe', speech to Britain in Europe, 23 November 1999.

13. Cook, *Point of Departure*, p. 103.

14. A. J. P. Taylor, *The Troublemakers: Dissent over Foreign Policy 1792–1939*, (London: Hamish Hamilton, 1957). The full text of Robin Cook's resignation speech can be found in Hansard, vol. 410, cols 726–8, and in the appendix of *Point of Departure*, pp. 361–5.

15. See Christopher Hill, 'Putting the World to Rights: Tony Blair's Foreign Policy Mission', in Anthony Seldon and Dennis Kavanagh (eds), *The Blair Effect 2001–5* (Cambridge: Cambridge University Press, 2005).

16. See William Wallace and Tim Oliver, 'A Bridge Too Far: Britain and the Transatlantic Alliance', in David Andrews (ed.), *The Atlantic Alliance under Stress: US–European Relations after Iraq* (Cambridge: Cambridge University Press, 2005).

17. See Bob Woodward, *Plan of Attack* (New York: Simon & Schuster, 2004).

18. Kampfner, *Blair's Wars*, p. 303.

19. W. G. Runciman (ed.), *Hutton and Butler: Lifting the Lid on the Workings of Power* (Oxford University Press, 2004).

20. See Peter Stothard, *30 Days: A Month at the Heart of Blair's War* (London: Harper Collins, 2003), p. 218.

21. 'A letter to Blair: Your Middle East policy is doomed, say diplomats', *Independent*, 27 April 2004.

22.   European Council, *A Secure Europe in a Better World: European Security Strategy*, December 2003.

23.   See John Dickie, *The New Mandarins: How British Foreign Policy Works* (London: I. B. Tauris, 2004).

24.   'MPs' report savages Foreign Office chief', *Guardian*, 8 March 2006.

25.   Tim Dunne, '"When the Shooting Starts": Atlanticism in British Security Strategy', *International Affairs* (2004), vol. 80, no. 5, 893–908.

26.   Seldon, *Blair*.

27   Ibid.

28.   Richard Heffernan, 'Prime Ministerial Predominance? Core Executive Politics in the UK', *British Journal of Politics and International Relations* (2003), vol. 5, no. 3.

29   See Mick Cox and Tim Oliver, 'Security Policy in an Insecure World', in Patrick Dunleavy, Richard Heffernan, Philip Cowley and Colin Hay (eds), *Developments in British Politics 8* (Basingstoke: Palgrave Macmillan, 2006).

30.   Seldon, *Blair*, p. 407.

31.   See John Micklethwait and Adrian Wooldridge, *The Right Nation: Conservative Power in America* (London: Penguin, 2004).

32.   Seldon, *Blair*, p. 624.

Index